NEW ORLEANS BEER

A HOPPY HISTORY OF BIG EASY BREWING

JEREMY LABADIE & ARGYLE WOLF-KNAPP

FOREWORD BY DAVID BLOSSMAN
INTRODUCTION BY KIRK COCO

AMERICAN PALATE

Published by American Palate
A Division of The History Press
Charleston, SC 29403
www.historypress.net

Cover image courtesy of Bill Cobb, skylinescenes.com.

First published 2014

Manufactured in the United States

ISBN 978.1.62619.248.5

Library of Congress CIP data applied for.

for Tree

for Aaron and Evangeline

But I didn't know how to write a book. So I wrote that down.
—*Max from* Freak the Mighty *by Rodman Philbrick*

CONTENTS

CONTENTS

FOREWORD

E verything old is new again.
    This book is about beer in New Orleans, past, present and future. I'm proud to say the Abita Brewing Company is an important part of this story.

As you'll learn, the growth of brewing in Louisiana is an exciting trend but not exactly new. In the 1850s, New Orleans was known as the "brewing capital of the South" with about fifty breweries listed in the city directory. Prohibition and the acquisition of small breweries by large ones pretty much killed beer innovation in New Orleans and all across the United States. But as we all know, you can't keep food and drink off the minds of Louisiana folks for very long, and beer is back in a big way.

The Abita Brewing Company was the first craft brewer in Louisiana, and what we set out to do was pretty radical at the time. When we started brewing in 1986, the only beer available was reminiscent of consumer choices in communist Russia—not much to choose from, and all of it bland. As home brewers, we wanted to enjoy beers that matched our culture and the way we love to live. Food in New Orleans is big, bold and tied into everything we do. So why shouldn't our beer be that way, too? Abita's full-flavored ales and lagers were a revolutionary idea. Consider this: two of our flagship brews, Abita Amber and Turbodog®, were considered "extreme" beers when they were first introduced; most people in Louisiana had never tasted anything like them. Beer styles have come a long way, and today craft brewing is booming in New Orleans. That's great news for beer drinkers, home brewers and breweries, too.

FOREWORD

Abita has always appreciated the rich history of brewing in New Orleans and how important beer is in our culture of food and fun. We've recently issued the second edition of our cookbook, *Cooking Louisiana True.* Our cookbook has short sections about the history of beer in New Orleans, but I'm very excited to read and learn even more about the history of our business in this great city and all the places to find and enjoy good beer. Jeremy has made a great contribution to the craft beer scene in New Orleans with his "Beer Buddha" blog, and Argyle's beer and food knowledge is amazing. Their talents have come together to create a valuable resource for the beer-drinking and brewing community, and we thank them for it.

Raise your glass to Jeremy and Argyle. Cheers for this noble effort!

DAVID BLOSSMAN
President, Abita Brewing Company
December 2013

PREFACE

Hi! We're Argyle and Jeremy, your hosts on this journey into the history of beer and brewing in New Orleans. We are both rather geekish beer lovers who got involved with putting this history together because a) we wanted to know about the subject and b) nobody had done it yet. So it fell to the two of us to put it together, despite us both being transplants to New Orleans. Our stories are here for you, just so you know with whom you're dealing. Enjoy!

JEREMY'S STORY: THE NEW ORLEANS BEER BUDDHA

Let me start by saying that I am not originally from New Orleans. I guess you can say I'm not originally from anywhere. Growing up a military brat, I moved around quite a bit. I've lived in Virginia, North Carolina, Hawaii, Rhode Island, Florida and, of course, New Orleans.

After having lived in so many American cities, I can honestly say there is nothing like New Orleans. This place is, without a doubt, the most unique town where I have ever had the pleasure of living. I moved here with my family in 1995, when my father was stationed at Tulane as the colonel who oversaw the naval ROTC. I met my wife in 1997 and have lived here ever since—with a couple sidetracks to other cities for work and, of course, that bitch Katrina.

PREFACE

I have long had a fascination with beer. When I was two, my father dressed me up as Billy Carter for Halloween, complete with a six-pack of cans. I can still remember my first beer ever. Sophomore year in high school, my best bud Randy Lenard thought it would be a great idea to get a marine to buy us beer from the local on-base C Store. It was a Colt .45 forty-ounce.

I still have the first beer bottle I purchased as a legal adult the day I turned twenty-one. It was a Dead Guy Ale from Rogue Brewery out of Ashland, Oregon, that I bought at a Sav-A-Center (now Rouses). Dead Guy was the beer that kick-started my exploration of beers—a great adventure that I am still on today.

I started writing about beer in early 2008, when I started working at a local wine store called Martin Wine Cellar. I had just been hired as an assistant manager and was interested in helping and working in the beer section. I felt that starting a beer blog would be a great idea to help promote not only the beer selection at Martin Wine Cellar but also craft beer here in the New Orleans area. The Beer Buddha was born.

Five years later, when The History Press approached me to write a book about the history of beer in New Orleans, I have to admit I was a bit shocked. I've never considered myself much of a writer. Blogger? Yes. Writer? No way. I write my blog the same way I would talk to you. I attempt to organize my thoughts and use punctuation, but most of the time I fail miserably. Either way, the folks at THP thought I was a good choice, but I knew I couldn't do it alone.

I knew of another gentleman named Argyle who had been working on putting together a history of beer in New Orleans for a tour he was interested in starting. It made sense to approach him about teaming up and working together on this project, and I'm truly glad I did! I feel he has tackled the history part of this book better than I could have.

The one important thing about this book is my approach. I wanted to write a book that I would want to read. I didn't want it to be some boring textbook-style beer book. This is a book about beer and New Orleans. Boring ain't gonna cut it.

This book is bigger than me. It represents an entire town—its people, past and present. I want this book to be a gift to my adopted city. I hope it is worthy. Sit back, grab a beer and enjoy!

Preface

Argyle's Story: The Great New Orleans Beer Tour

In the summer of 2006, my wife, Sondra, and I moved to New Orleans. I had wanted to visit for years, mostly because of the music. I was born and raised on San Francisco traditional jazz, growing up on a diet of Lu Watters, Bob Scobey, Turk Murphy, Clancy Heyes and the Firehouse 5. San Francisco traditional jazz is a musically miniscule step from New Orleans; the cities have a lot in common once you get past the topography. While Hurricane Katrina had torn the city apart the year before we came, destruction leads to growth, and Sondra got a job offer from the University of New Orleans. I couldn't believe my good luck.

While getting to know our new city, I saw the Jax Brewery, just off Jackson Square. It was the home of the Jackson Brewing Company, built in 1890.[1] It's just a shopping mall now—more's the pity. Jax had gone out of business in 1974, selling the name and formula to the Pearl Brewing Company of San Antonio, Texas.[2] I had known about Jax and Dixie before moving here and found out about the Falstaff plant (now being converted into condominiums) shortly afterward. The city used to have an identity as a brewing center, but in 2006, the only commercial brewing being done here was at the Crescent City and Gordon Biersch brewpubs. This puzzled me a bit, although I figured that Hurricane Katrina was in part to blame; it certainly had been for Dixie.

But life goes on. Sondra had a solid academic position, and I wound up with a good job at the famed Commander's Palace restaurant in the Garden District. We settled into the rhythms of the city, working hard and catching as much live, local music as we could. Life was good.

In early 2012, a co-worker of mine named Tree* asked for a favor. He has a business[3] as a tour guide and wanted to get some objective feedback on his Garden District tour. So I took his tour. There were a few things I felt he needed to address, and we discussed them afterward over a couple beers. Outside of my nitpicking, Tree had given a great tour and shown why he is as well regarded as he is. I found myself beginning to entertain thoughts about eventually doing something similar; after all, fine-dining waiting is hard work, and I wasn't getting any younger. The thought of creating an easier job just waiting for me to retire into began to look appealing.

Most tours of New Orleans are cultural (pirates, houses, graveyards, vampires and such), but it is commerce and industry that shape cities. I asked

---

* Really—that's his entire name.

13

Tree if he had ever considered giving any tours dealing with the industrial history of New Orleans; Tree in turn asked me what I wanted to know. When I mentioned brewing history, Tree said that he didn't know much about it and suggested that I should research it. Tree also said he would be more than happy to help set up a tour when the information was put together.

So with visions of creating the Great New Orleans Beer Tour, I hit the books—only to find that nothing comprehensive on the topic had been written. I found lots of newspaper articles, ordinances and civic notices in the historical archives but nothing comprehensive. Online, I found several brewing memorabilia sites, some of which also deal in books and other source material. One such site is run by the Eastern Coast Breweriana Association (ECBA); I bought a copy of *American Breweries II*,[4] by Dale P. Van Wieren, from it. This book claims to list every brewery registered in the United States (state by state) from 1612 until 1995, when the book was published.* This claim is slightly exaggerated, but it's a good starting point. The ECBA site also led me to a hilarious article on the first air shipment of beer, which was made by the Lemp Brewing Company of St. Louis to the mayor of New Orleans back in 1912. It's reprinted here courtesy of Kevin Kious.

Using the New Orleans data in *American Breweries II*, I began building a map[5] (using Google Maps) showing all of the breweries that had been in New Orleans since 1851 (the Brasserie was started here in 1726,† but *American Breweries II* does not list it). Then the fun began as data tables ran headfirst into reality. The first problem I ran into was the numbering of streets in New Orleans, which has been redone more than once, most recently in 1894. Every address in *American Breweries II* is from the time of each brewery's operation, which in most cases meant that the addresses were obsolete—sometimes just renumbered, sometimes gone from the face of the earth. I went to both Tulane University's library and the Historical New-Orleans Collection for further research and was introduced to the Sanborn Fire Insurance Company maps of New Orleans, the first of which came out in 1893. I was also directed to the *Robinson Atlas* of 1883. These maps not only had the addresses of the time but also showed the actual footprints of

---

* That first brewery, just so you know, was located at the southern tip of Manhattan Island and was owned and operated by Adrian Block and Hans Christiansen from 1612 until 1632. Jean Vigne, the first nonnative American born in the New Amsterdam colony, was born in the brewery in 1614. He grew up to become a brewer himself.

† That's the earliest date I have found for a brewery in New Orleans.

the buildings. *Gardner's Directory of New Orleans* (1866) also had a surprise: it lists the Heen Brewery, which *American Breweries II* didn't do. This led to other historical directories of New Orleans and still more breweries.

The second problem I encountered was the renaming of some streets, which also has been done more than once in some cases. The *Robinson Atlas* resolved many of these issues. The third problem was the reformation of the city waterfront itself due to levee* and port facility development. Several locations were thus rendered ambiguous; some no longer exist. A few were listed by intersection rather than street number, which usually made finding them a bit easier.[6]

After mapping all the historical brewery sites, I created a walking tour of some sites in the Marigny District, a loop that can be walked in under an hour and passes the sites of seven breweries, beginning and ending at the Crescent City Brewhouse. I then drove this tour route and found out that this was going to be a bit surreal: of these seven brewery sites, only Jax is still standing. The only traces that remain are on the maps; there are none on the ground. This same issue came up on the other tour routes I was contemplating.

The breweries of New Orleans are fairly scattered, and getting around to see more than a few poses problems on foot, in terms of both human effort and time. Thus, for a comprehensive tour, a vehicle is called for. The previous summer in Munich, I had seen a Beer Bike:[7] a four-wheel, pedal-powered vehicle seating fifteen, with six seats on each side facing one another, two at the back facing forward and a designated driver in front. There's also a central well area for a bartender and a keg. The well is enclosed by a narrow bar with holes to hold cups at each seat. I began to think of just how much fun it would be to give a tour to a group of folks on such a bike—touring beer sites with beer on tap![8] Tree seemed even more excited by this prospect than I was and doubtless thought of other tours that could be done this way. However, given New Orleans' justifiably notorious permitting process, it seems unlikely that the Great New Orleans Beer Tour will ever happen on a bike. A bus tour is in the works.

In the course of mapmaking and writing up the tour talks, I realized that I was writing the book I hadn't been able to find about this history. So I began the process of turning it into a book. Eventually I met Jeremy, who was working on the same thing. We thought that combining our efforts would result in a better situation all around, and so here we are.

---

* This is still going on, most recently on Algiers Point.

PREFACE

New Orleans is best known by its neighborhoods. With this in mind, I've split this history into six parts along geographic lines. (There is also a time line of the industry as a whole so you can get a sense of the overall picture.) These six areas are the French Quarter; Marigny and the Bywater; Tremé and Storyville; the lower Central Business District (CBD from here on) and Algiers; Uptown (which includes the former cities of Lafayette and Jefferson and the town of Carrollton); and Mid-City. Each of these areas developed somewhat independently of the others (in roughly this order), and touring each area by itself is more feasible than touring the entire city at once.

We'll begin with an overview of beer in America and then get into the heart of the matter, beginning with the French Quarter—both because that's where this party started and because that's what an awful lot of people think is the entirety of New Orleans. (They're wrong but numerous...)

ACKNOWLEDGEMENTS

JEREMY'S THANKS

I'd like to thank the following people:

My wife, Aaron, and my daughter, Evangeline. Thanks for all the support you have given! Without y'all's support, none of this would have been possible. And see, honey, I told you that drinking beer could pay off one day.

My mom, dad and brother Jordan. You built the foundation for the Beer Buddha to grow on. Especially my dad, who dressed me up as Billy Carter for Halloween in 1977.

My in-laws Pat and Desha for producing such a beautiful daughter and allowing me to marry her. You guys have always been there for both of us. It is truly appreciated!

Randy Lenard for getting us those Colt .45s.

Christen Thompson and The History Press for somehow seeing something in me that screamed I should write a book for you.

Polly Adler and Dan Stein. Thank you so much for everything you do for craft beer in New Orleans.

Greg Hackenberg—I told you I'd put your name in here. Thanks for the help you provided. Not sure I would have found La Brasserie on my own...

The band Galactic, for providing me with a soundtrack to this book. Every time I worked on this book, it was Galactic I was listening to.

In addition, I would like to thank Jim Durbin, John Coker, Nora McGunnigle, Jarrett Fosberg, Brenton Day, Jay and Eric Ducote, Kirk

Coco and the rest of the NOLA Brewing gang, everyone at Bayou Teche, David Blossman, Leo Basile and the rest of the gang at Abita Brewery, Leith Adams from Mudbug Brewing, Jason Sanner, Vasu Tamala, bacon for being so delicious, beer (of course) and, finally, my high school principal, who basically told me that I'd never amount to anything but be a marine like my father (like somehow that'd be a bad thing).

If I left anyone out, I am truly sorry. It wasn't on purpose. I've been drinking. A lot.

ARGYLE'S THANKS

Some thanks are in order:

I am extremely grateful to the excellent research staff and facilities at Tulane University, the New Orleans Public Library and the Historic New-Orleans Collection's Williams Research Center, whose records have made it possible to sort out the information to the degree to which I have done. The importance of the Sanborn Fire Insurance Company maps (1893, 1896 and 1909, mostly) and the *Robinson Atlas* of 1883 to this project cannot be overstated.

The fact that my ever-loving wife, Sondra (who doesn't care for beer at all!), has put up with and encouraged this obsession of mine is a source of wonder to me. Thanks, love. Dale P. Van Wieren's book *American Breweries II* provided the bulk of my base data concerning dates and addresses of the various breweries. Stan Schneider of Baton Rouge shared his family's remembrances of the Union Brewery and gave me much encouragement early on. Jennifer Navarre of the Historic New-Orleans Collection introduced me to the Sanborn maps, without which this project would have been pretty much impossible to do. Both Eira Tansey and Sean Benjamin at Tulane University's Howard-Tilton Library Rare Book Room shepherded me through historical documentation of the changing streets of New Orleans, as well as introducing me to the *Robinson Atlas of New Orleans*. Mike Calabrese also clarified some issues I had concerning locations and street names. *Gambit* magazine's "Blake Pontchartrain" answer column provided information about the Weckerling and American Breweries (unfortunately, these columns are no longer available unless you have the particular issue in your possession). The New Orleans Notarial Archives still has contractual records for all of the breweries (and all other legitimate New Orleans businesses as well, for that matter) and their respective builders and provides a keen insight into how things work down here, for better and worse.* Peter "Hopzilla" Caddoo and Kirk Coco of NOLA Brewing provided inspiration, insights and camaraderie. Amy Loewy of the Garden District Book Shop deserves special thanks for keeping me concise. The interest and enthusiasm of my colleagues at Commander's Palace has been phenomenal. You all have my thanks and profound gratitude.

Special thanks are also due to Christen Thompson and The History Press for bringing this project to fruition.

So what you have here in your hand is the history of brewing in New Orleans as best I can put it together, as well as a guide to visiting the remaining sites, should you care to do so. My mistakes are my own, and I really can't thank those who have inspired and helped me along the way anywhere near enough.

And Tree, thanks again for getting me into this in the first place. It's been a heck of a fun ride.

---

* The worst part was the discovery that all the records filed are under the name of the notary who filed them, not the parties to the documents or the properties involved. It is a system that hinders clarity, to say the least...

INTRODUCTION

History. Culture. Tradition. These are the cornerstones of the city of New Orleans, known to foreigners as the "Big Easy" but to natives as the "City that Care Forgot" or the "Crescent City." We are proud of a multicultural history that includes starting as a Native American meeting point and settlement and then becoming part of France, Spain, the United States of America and, for a brief period, the Confederate States of America before returning to our current American rule. Of course, we are New Orleanians first. Much of the history of each of the above rulers was changed forever by this river city, the "Pearl of the Gulf."

Our unique culture is why we identify so closely with our city. Jazz funerals, Mardi Gras, music festivals—hell, *everything* festivals—happen every day of the week, and in this city you never have to search for something to do but simply regret all the things you'll miss by doing something else. If New York is the city that never sleeps, New Orleans is the city with people who never sleep. We are too busy to take the time out.

Tradition also plays a large part in our daily lives. Compounded by the Catholic and Jewish religious rites of most families in the city, there is always a ritual and ceremony to everything we do. From pouring absinthe, taking a shot, burying the dead, eating King cake or ordering a po'boy, everyone in this city has special rituals that make these seemingly everyday acts religious occasions, as well as uniquely personal ones. I have my own particular way to drink a beer that I never stray from, and most everyone will tell you his or her own traditions for any action you could endeavor. And all of them are, of course, *correct*.

INTRODUCTION

Brewing began early on in the city's history and thrived in our festive culture. As the city continues to rebuild its brewing industry into its former fame as the "Brewing Capital of the South," we continue to look back, as all good New Orleanians do. We strive to grow our new industry in line with the history behind us, in tune with our unique culture and building on the tradition of the wonderful breweries, personalities and beers in which you are about to enthrall yourself through reading this book.

As your tour guides, you have the two people I would personally want with me if I could go back in time and see it all for myself. Jeremy "Beer Buddha" Labadie is a close friend and companion whom I have known since the beginning of my experience with the brewing industry here in New Orleans and probably my first choice with whom to quaff multiple pints of every conceivable fermented beverage. His knowledge of craft beer is insurmountable, and yet he will just as willingly kill a six-pack of PBR with you on a hot night at a crawfish boil.

Argyle's knowledge of food and drink is legendary, and as an entertaining conversationalist and keeper of strange and interesting facts, he is the perfect person to fill the breaks while we are too busy killing beers to speak. Understanding the crucial interplay between beer and food, he would definitely be picking the pairings we would try on our journey.

So let these two time travelers take you from the first brewery in our city all the way to today's burgeoning craft beer scene, and pour yourself a beer to set the stage for one of the most interesting reads you will ever embark upon.

KIRK COCO

PART I

L'HISTOIRE

CHAPTER 1

A SHORT HISTORY OF BEER IN NEW ORLEANS AND AMERICA

Beer has been with us from the very start of the country. It's been said—with some accuracy—that our revolution against England was born in the taverns. Taverns were the social heart of the colonies, and most of them made their own beer. These taverns served mostly English-style beers, ales and porters, as lager beer was not yet made here and was expensive to import. Breweries as we think of them have been in operation here since 1612,[9] but large breweries weren't the norm until much later on. The rise of lager beer in America (and by extension, the larger production breweries necessary for it) appears to have been the natural result of three primary factors converging: ethnic German immigration to the New World, advancement in naval design in the form of clipper ships and the development of artificial refrigeration and ice making.

The first half of the 1800s saw several waves of German immigration to the United States. This was for both economic and religious reasons; the final wave (1846–56) was primarily due to a potato famine.[10] The U.S. census of 1850 shows the German population of New Orleans as 11,425; the total population was 116, 375.[11] This roughly 10 percent mark seems to have been a sort of tipping point for social impact. These newer immigrants stayed mostly in and around New Orleans, joining the extant German community. Earlier German immigrants had settled in the Côte des Allemandes district upriver; many eventually moved to New Orleans. This led to an increased demand for beer in the city.

Prior to 1842, the only way to get lager beer in the New World was to import it from Europe. Lager beer is different from ale,* most notably in terms of its stability. The ales and porters of the time tended to be a bit unstable and were rather subject to souring, especially in hot weather. Thus, they were best made in small batches and consumed soon after being made. For home and small-tavern production, this isn't a problem, and there was a thriving market in "city beer"† as well. Lagering, on the other hand, takes longer to do; it is made by a hybrid species of yeast and needs cooler temperatures to work well. Lager is more suited to larger-scale production and both stores and ships better than traditional ales. (There is also a category of lager called *schenk*, which is fermented at warmer temperatures than true lager. Like city beer, it's meant for immediate consumption.)

Clipper ships were designed to provide speedy transit, and they did. While the 3,804-mile journey from Bremen to New York took ten to fifteen days by paddle wheeler, a clipper could do it in six to seven days with the right winds. One of the byproducts of this reduced transit time was a lower cost of transport, which made the Europe–America trade routes more affordable. Importing lager also brought lager yeast to the New World. With a viable lager yeast culture to work with, lager beer could be made here, and Frederick and Maximilian Schafer did just that in 1842. Their beer went on to become the largest-selling beer in the world.[12] By 1851, lager was being brewed here throughout the Northeast and Great Lakes regions.

Additionally, there was a booming cotton trade between New Orleans and Bremen. The clipper ships offered competitive fares for immigrants to America (it costs less to feed someone for one week than for two, and this allowed for lower fares), resulting in New Orleans becoming more of a U.S. destination of choice for many. People to America, cotton to Europe—a nice two-leg trade route.

Until the development of artificial refrigeration, professional brewing was mostly a fall-to-spring occupation. In higher latitudes, caves and cellaring

---

* See Part II, "Ale and Lager Beer 101."

† A word about "city beer." This was found throughout the colonies (later on, states). It was a beer made of whatever grains were available and frequently flavored (and sweetened) with molasses; it is still made today (Parish Brewing's Canebrake is a great example of it). Barley was known to be the best grain for this, but corn was a major component as well, and any other grains might be used as the brewer saw fit. Hops were sometimes used, sometimes not. The practice of using a blend of herbs was common—the exact herbs being a choice of the brewer. Hops and barley were relatively expensive, and brewing is fraught with managing fractions of pennies on ingredients.

tunnels were used for brewing operations to extend the season, although that isn't an option in New Orleans. The brewing season could also be extended by using ice, but this was not cheap—especially in the tropics. There were some who made their fortunes in shipping ice from the North (Frederic Tudor, notably),[13] and icehouses were certainly useful,[14] but the cost could be daunting, especially for a new business.

Artificial ice making was first developed by Dr. John Gorrie, of Apalachicola, Florida.* His design (U.S. Patent 8080[15], granted on May 6, 1851) was intended to produce ice to be used in cooling the air for malaria patients. While his machine worked, it was unreliable and subject to breakage. Subsequent inventors developed more efficient methods based on his research, using first ether and then ammonia instead of compressed air. In 1869, refrigeration equipment was installed in George Merz's Old Canal Brewery at Toulouse and Villere Streets. That refrigeration equipment was designed by Charles Tellier,[16] and Merz had modest success with it. With artificial refrigeration, the seasonal aspect of brewing became a thing of the past, although seasonal beers are still made to this day. The only difference is that now they can be made at any time the brewer chooses rather than at the dictates of the season. (Whether this is a good thing is up for debate.)

By this time, there was a thriving trade in domestic lager beer to New Orleans from the North. According to Ellen C. Merrill in her 2005 book *The Germans of Louisiana*, the first shipments of domestic lager beer to New Orleans arrived from the Schenk Brewery of Pittsburgh, Pennsylvania, in 1851[17]† and were sold by Christian Krost in his coffeehouse (read "tavern" for "coffeehouse"—this was typical for the time). This had the happy side effect of providing the city with live lager yeast cultures. This in turn enabled local brewers to produce *schenk* (and eventually lagers) in addition to the ales and porters they had been making.

---

* There's a lovely, if small, museum dealing with Gorrie's work in Apalachicola, at the intersection of Sixth Street and Avenue D, just off Route 98. It costs two dollars to get in and is open 10:00 a.m. to 5:00 p.m. Thursdays through Mondays. Copies of his patent are available for sale.

† Unfortunately, I can't verify this. There are three Schenk breweries listed in American Breweries II, located in Nauvoo, Illinois; Warrensburg, Missouri; and St. Joseph, Missouri. None of these was in operation in 1851. There were ten other breweries operating in Pittsburgh then, though, and schenk is also a type of beer made with lager yeast but fermented at warmer temperatures than lager would be. It was made for immediate consumption, like ales and porters, and is probably what Merrill is referring to.

To say that New Orleans embraced lager would be a gross understatement; then, as now, good beer has a place near and dear to our hearts. The Lemp Brewing Co. of St. Louis, Missouri,* began shipping to New Orleans in the early 1850s, beginning a relationship with the city that has lasted well over a century. Anheuser-Busch also shipped its beer here, and while it never brewed here, the company built a distribution warehouse at the base of Common Street. All of these breweries had to contend with the weather during river transit, of course. Quite a bit of beer was lost to both freezing barrels in the winter and exploding ones in the summer.[18]

With these various factors in place, lager brewing in New Orleans began in earnest, augmenting the existing ale and porter brewing. Over the next half century, many people tried the business. Most of them failed. These failures were due to any number of reasons, from inept accounting to competition to fire (and in 1920, Prohibition). Toward the end of the nineteenth century, brewery consolidation became a major business factor as well, as larger breweries bought smaller ones to both eliminate competition and expand their own production. This was not just a domestic phenomenon. Several English brewing syndicates were looking to buy American breweries to expand their market shares. (That practice is still going on today, which is why Budweiser is now owned and operated by the Brazil- and Belgium-based company Anheuser-Busch InBev.)[19] The New Orleans Brewing Association was created in 1890 to combat this practice, as for someone to buy the association would mean having to buy six relatively large breweries at once.

One other major factor in the history of beer was Prohibition,[20] the culmination of the temperance movement. This was a social-engineering experiment on a national level and had many unintended side effects, among them the rise of organized crime, a statistically significant level of female alcoholism, massive levels of unemployment and (later on) dry counties and NASCAR. The original goal of the temperance movement was laudable. Temperance advocates saw the consumption of alcohol, especially in the form of distilled spirits, as a social ill that wrecked lives. They initially advocated moderation in alcohol consumption (hence the term "temperance" as opposed to "abstinence") and held beer and wine to be healthy beverages. Brewers initially supported this, as they saw temperance advocates to be their allies against the distillers in the battle for the drinking man's dollar. We all know how that turned out.

---

* Lemp beer was renamed Falstaff in the 1870s.

While Prohibition made alcohol production and sales illegal, enforcement was quite another matter, and the stories are legion.* Supposedly, in 1921, an inspector was sent from Washington to New Orleans to verify that Prohibition was being enforced. He was able to get directions to a speakeasy within fifteen seconds of getting into a cab at Union Station. While this story may be apocryphal (there are many variants out there and not only in New Orleans), it really shows the heart of the matter. Cultural hospitality norms here meant that while lip service to the Prohibition laws might have to be paid, enforcement wasn't going to happen without reoccupying the city with an army.

Prohibition lasted nearly fourteen years, ending on December 5, 1933, with the ratification of the Twenty-first Amendment.† Booze went back on sale the next day (notably Dewar's Scotch—they planned well), and we went about getting life back to normal. Two of the biggest changes after Prohibition were the elimination of the "tied house"[21] system and the creation of the three-tier system of alcohol distribution.‡

Another major effect of the Twenty-first Amendment was the gradual reemployment of brewery workers. It was estimated that one in ten jobs in the United States had been brewery related in 1910. Prohibition had created tremendous unemployment. The landscape of the industry had changed, of course—well over half the active breweries that existed before Prohibition had gone bankrupt. There was a rush to restart the industry but, in many cases, by folks who had no clue how to run a brewery.

One of the larger factors in the early post-Prohibition brewing industry seems to have been turnover—short-lived breweries succeeded by other

---

* One such story was told to me by my boss at Commander's Palace. It seems that a great-uncle of his wound up employed as a night watchman for a distillery on the West Bank. He had come to New Orleans from Kentucky to work in the distillery, but when Prohibition shuttered it, he became the guy in charge of making sure that nothing went in or out. One night, the distillery was broken into. The burglars put him into a rowboat without oars and set him adrift in the middle of the Mississippi River to keep him out of the way. The booze was gone by morning; he was rescued somewhere well downriver the following morning.
† Why December 5 is still not a national holiday eludes me.
‡ Not counting brewpubs, current U.S. federal law makes it illegal for a brewery to own a tavern or to sell its beer to anyone but a licensed distributor. Breweries can give out free samples of their beer, but they cannot sell it directly to a consumer. They must sell it to a distributor, who in turn must sell it to a retailer who sells it to you. Wineries and distilleries are exempt from this restriction and can sell directly to people. (Please note that Louisiana now permits breweries to sell up to 10 percent of their beer on-site directly to the public.)

short-lived breweries. The only ones who did well in this environment were the equipment manufacturers, malt producers and larger breweries that had survived Prohibition. This last group went about buying even more capacity to brew, and a newer model of business came to dominate the national landscape. This model was based on going for the lowest price to increase market share without regard to regional style or seasonality. This became even more pronounced during World War II, with lighter American pilsner[*] becoming the default preferred national style. This style was initially aimed at the female factory worker market in particular, just as filtered cigarettes were. The success of American pilsner was due to market concentration, with most of the big breweries making variants of the same style and little else; lots of advertising; low prices; and a fading demand for older, more full-flavored traditional beers. An unhappy byproduct of this style dominance was fierce competition between makers of similar products, which made price the single most powerful variable for the market. The consolidation of the brewing industry that flowed from that is similar to Microsoft's consolidation of software in more recent times and has deep effects to this day.[†]

With demand for more full-flavored beers declining, fewer of them were made, which made them harder to find, which in turn decreased demand even more—a vicious cycle. By 1970, only one brewery in America (Narragansett, owned by Falstaff, in Cranston, Rhode Island) was still making porter (although this began to change in rather short order, beginning with Anchor in San Francisco). If you wanted a bigger, bolder beer, you had to either make it yourself (which was still illegal) or buy imports. Prohibition had almost destroyed a culinary demand for traditional beers. But that's a tale for another day, and we've got a city to explore.

---

[*] Coors, Olympia, Pabst, Hamm's, Falstaff, Schlitz and Budweiser are the most obvious.
[†] Which is why we have actual serious debates over the relative merits of Bud Light, Miller Lite and Coors Light. Pheh.

Chapter 2

THE BREWERIES OF NEW ORLEANS, THE BREWING CAPITAL OF THE OLD SOUTH

THE FIRST NEW ORLEANS BREWERY

First and foremost was the Brasserie, which opened in 1726 in what is now the Bywater section of old New Orleans. The Brasserie was the first plantation downriver from the Marigny Plantation,[22] running roughly from Franklin Avenue to Press Street and from the river to the edge of the swamp.[23] It was owned by Pierre Dreux and his brother, Mathurin. It was not a brasserie as we know them today—a restaurant that brews its own beer (a brewpub by any other name); rather, it was a plantation that made its money by supplying beer to Nouvelle Orleans. In December 1728, M. Dreux brought suit in the Nouvelle Orleans Supreme Council against one M. Decoeur for nonpayment regarding 131 livres of beer, which Dreux had provided. M. Decoeur thus has the distinction of being the first recorded deadbeat to skip out on a bar tab in New Orleans. In 1743, Pierre Dreux's widow, Anne, sold the Brasserie to a Villars Debreuil, who owned the adjacent property downriver. Debreuil's granddaughter Felicity inherited it in 1751 and eventually sold it to Don Bernardo de Galvez (the Spanish governor) in 1777. The next brewery in the Bywater was built in 1872, but we'll get to that later on.

Breweries of the French Quarter

The first brewery in the French Quarter appears to have been the Stadtsbreuerei (City Brewery), which was opened in 1845 at "Philip and Royal" by two men (Wirth and Fischer), according to a city directory of the time.[24] We have found no record of when it went out of business.

The first recorded shipments of lager to New Orleans arrived in 1851.[25] This was actually a shipment of *schenk* beer (lager beer fermented at warmer temperatures than true lager and meant for immediate consumption rather than aging), which was contracted for and sold by Christian Krost at his coffeehouse (read "tavern"). About the same time, George Guth opened his Louisiana Brewery at 85 (now 805) Conti Street. The building there now has a door at 805 with a "Rex Room" sign on it, which appears to be a private back entrance to the Jester's Daiquiri shop on the corner. The brewery was quite small by today's standards but ran well enough to last until 1861. The exact reasons for closing down are unclear, although the Civil War and the threat of Union occupation may have been considerations. The city's economy was booming throughout the 1850s, but the war put a serious damper on it.

In 1854, Joseph Christen opened a small brewery at 46 (now 632) St. Philip Street, quite possibly in the same facility that had been the Stadtsbreuerei. He ran it here until 1857, when he moved operations to a new facility in the Marigny at 104 Moreau Street. We'll get back to him later on.

While Christen was moving in 1857, the Gottwald Brewery opened at 125 (now 1033) St. Philip Street. It was a short-lived operation, closing in 1860. This was probably due to increasing competition as much as anything. Even with a growing population (from 116,375 in 1850 to 168,165 in 1860—an increase of over 40 percent), there were five other breweries in the city, and the river trade was flourishing.

In 1860, Karl Krost opened his brewery at 51 (now 625) Conti Street. He lasted until only 1861—again, probably due (at least in part) to the war. As is the case with the vast majority of the older breweries here, there's nothing left of Krost's at all today. The area was a tenement slum and was subjected to urban renewal in 1908. Every building on the block was demolished, and by 1910, a new Supreme Court building stood there, taking up the whole block.[26]

Over the next thirty years, several breweries opened throughout the city, although not in the French Quarter proper. In 1890, two important developments in the local brewing industry took place. First was the formation of the New Orleans Brewing Association by Peter Blaise, J.J.

Weckerling and several others. This association was formed to consolidate the major breweries of New Orleans to make it difficult, if not impossible, for outsiders to purchase them. In this case, there was an English brewing syndicate interested in purchasing breweries here to get into the American market. It was looking elsewhere in America as well and did buy several breweries in other parts of the country. NOBA was simply too expensive for the Brits, so the consolidation strategy seems to have worked. The second development was the opening of the Jackson Brewery on Decatur Street by Lawrence Fabacher. In addition to Jackson beer, it produced Fabacher, Bohemian Hof-Brau, Tex, 4-X and Sabana beer. In 1956, the Fabachers acquired the copyright to the Jax name from the Jax Brewing Company of Jacksonville, Florida,[27] when it went out of business. Within a decade, the renamed Jax Brewery had grown to become the tenth-highest-producing brewery in the United States.

This was a short-lived period of prosperity, however. In 1970, it was purchased by Meisterbrau and then, in 1974, went out of business, selling the Jax name to the Pearl Brewing Company of San Antonio, Texas. Pearl continued to produce Jax until 1985, when it was bought by the Pabst Brewing Company. In 2001, Pearl was shut down, and Jax passed into history. Pearl beer is still being brewed under contract by Miller Brewing at its Fort Worth facility, as Dixie is still brewed under contract with the Minhas Craft brewery in Monroe, Wisconsin. Part of the Pearl brewing complex has since been

The former Jax Brewery is now an upscale shopping center. A small shrine to its brewing heyday still exists on the second floor. *Argyle Wolf-Knapp.*

turned into apartments; some the main buildings have been remade into a campus (the third) for the Culinary Institute of America. The Jax facility in Jacksonville has been turned into a local museum, with an annual Jax Beer Week festival (usually in early April). The Jax Brewery here in New Orleans is just a shopping mall now, with a small museum on the second floor.

In 1891, the American Brewing Company opened operations on most of the block bordered by Bourbon, Conti, Royal and Bienville Streets. The facility had been the home of the New Orleans Claret Company (a wine importing and bottling concern) before that. American brewed Regal Beer, among others, and its jingle—"Red beans and rice and Regal on ice!"—and the visage of its trademark, "Prince Regal," saluting the public were ubiquitous in the South. During Prohibition, it brewed near-beer and soft drinks. After Prohibition, it went back to producing Regal Beer, Regal Ale and Toby Porter. American expanded by buying other brewing facilities (the Wagner Brewery in Granite City, Illinois,[28] in January 1939 and Standard in 1947, among others) but ultimately could not compete on a national level. In 1962, it went out of business. The building was renovated in 1964;[29] the Royal Sonesta Hotel is there now.

A building with Jax and Regal signs. *John Frances Benjamin, Library of Congress, Prints & Photographs Division, LC-DIG-csas-01301.*

In 1908, the People's Brewery (also called the People's CO-OP Brewery) opened at 610 Bienville Street. This was the second time the People's name was used; it closed up shop in 1909.

Three years later, the Union Brewery opened at 129 Decatur Street. In 1919, it moved its operations to a new fireproof, four-story facility at 2809–29 North Robertson Street at Press Street. It produced Union Beer and Old Union Ale and (oddly enough for a beer named Union here in the heart of Dixie) enjoyed a very good reputation. (More on Union later, in the Marigny section.)

The year 1920 brought Prohibition. This social experiment killed off most of the brewing industry, although some breweries survived by making soft drinks and malt products (malt powder for malted milk, for instance). The social impact of Prohibition cannot be overstated. The mindset that brought it about is still very much alive and well today. It's enough to give one pause concerning societal experimentation.

While Prohibition ended in 1933 (ratified on December 5—a cause to celebrate!), no other breweries opened in the French Quarter until 1991. That was the Crescent City Brewhouse,[30] opened by Wolfram Koehler at 527 Decatur Street, just two blocks from Jax. It produces four staple beers (Pilsner; Red Stallion, a Vienna-style beer; Black Forest, a Munich-style *dunkle*; and an unfiltered Weiss), plus seasonal offerings, and is doing great business.

BREWERIES OF THE TREMÉ AND STORYVILLE

For those who are unfamiliar with New Orleans, the Tremé is the section of the city immediately lakeward of the French Quarter, roughly between Rampart and Roman Streets from Canal to Esplanade Streets. It was developed as part of the early expansion of the city and was historically a free black neighborhood, one of the oldest in the country. Storyville (also known as "the District") is the section of Tremé bounded by Basin, North Robertson, Iberville and St. Louis Streets. It was named after Sidney Story, an alderman, who wrote legislation in 1897 designating it as a red-light district.[31] Some studies done in Europe suggested that having a designated section for prostitution was preferable to having prostitutes going about all over the town, and so the District was created. This status was revoked in 1917 due to concerns expressed by the army and navy after four soldiers were killed there. The closing of the District was protested by New Orleans officials, including the mayor, Martin Behrman, who is on record as saying, "You can make it illegal, but you can't make it unpopular." The biggest effects of this closing were to drive the gambling dens underground and raise the price of prostitutes.

Five breweries were built in the Tremé over the years, although none was active in Storyville during its heyday. The first was the Coffeehouse & Brewery, which was opened by George Merz in 1858. It was on the uptown riverside corner of Villere and Toulouse Streets. Given that the brewery was right on the Carondelet Canal, shipping was probably a large part of the business; indeed, it thrived and was renamed the Old Canal Brewery & Coffeehouse in 1866. Merz was one of the more innovative brewers in New Orleans and was willing to gamble earlier than most with newer technologies. In 1865, he installed a steam engine to power the brewery and mechanized most of the operations, thus cutting his labor costs. This was written about by a local paper:

> *The engine is sixteen horsepower. It can, at the same time, grind the malt, sift it, throw it into the mash tub, let in boiling water that it has made to boil, stir up the malt and water, draw it off, pump it upstairs and throw it into the kettle, heat the kettle of liquid until it boils, throw it out into the coolers, cool it, force and carry it off into vats, ferment it, chafe it, and draw it off beer. With a little practice, the engine could be taught to drink the beer.[32]*

In 1868, the Coffeehouse part of the name was removed. In 1869, Merz installed the first mechanical refrigeration equipment ever put into a brewery. This was designed by Charles Tellier and was powered by the same steam engine that ran the rest of the brewery. While the engine worked out fine, the refrigeration equipment had some issues and eventually was refitted to produce ice, as it couldn't provide sufficient direct air conditioning.

Merz also ran Magnolia Garden, a German beer garden on Bayou St. John,[33] on the point of land bounded by Moss Street, Harding Drive and Dumaine Street. Despite these successes, he went out of business in 1878 (perhaps due, in part, to the yellow fever epidemic of that year). The last record I can find of him is from 1879; his nephew Valentine went on to become a major force in the industry.

In 1869, the Marais Street Steam Brewery was opened by H.F. Strarchen at 86 (now 410) Marais Street, on the corner of Marais and Conti Streets. It stayed in business until 1886. It's the only brewery site within the Storyville area proper and is not a safe place to visit. The site is now part of the Iberville housing project; no trace of the brewery remains.

In 1870, the Pelican Brewery was opened at 282 (now 1230) Villere Street by Phillip Wirtz, with the bottling works on the lake side of the street. In 1887, it was bought by Eugene Erath and moved to a much larger facility on the river side of Chartres Street, between Louisa and Clouet Streets.

In 1882, the Southern Brewery was opened on the site of the Old Canal Brewery. Southern was a much larger operation, covering most of a city block. The bottling works were across St. Louis Street. Southern merged into the New Orleans Brewing Association in 1890 and went out of business in 1900. The building is long gone now; the site is currently occupied by the Vieux Carré RV Park.

In 1887, the Crescent Brewing Company opened on the block bordered by Canal Street, Claiborne Avenue, Iberville and North Robertson Streets, taking the entire block. The block had previously been the main location of Wood's cotton press; Wood also owned half of the next block toward the river. In 1890, Crescent merged with the New Orleans Brewing Association. Yet for all of its size and capacity, it was shut down just two years later and eventually demolished. Coca-Cola took over most of the facility as a bottling works and, by 1940, was sharing the block with an auto dealership, an auto painting shop and a filling station on the corner of Canal and Claiborne. The site is currently a center for Louisiana Family Support Services.

BREWERIES OF THE MARIGNY AND BYWATER

The Marigny District was one of the earliest expansions of New Orleans from the original garrison grid that we know today as the French Quarter. It was developed in 1806 by Bernard Xavier Philippe de Marigny de Mandeville, who had inherited the land from his father, Pierre Philippe de Marigny de Mandeville.[34] It is bounded by Esplanade to the west and Franklin Avenue to the east from the river to Claiborne Avenue. (The Brasserie had been on the section of land between Franklin and Press and was subsumed into an enlarged Marigny after the Spanish gave the colony back to France.) The section of the city immediately east/downstream from the Marigny is the Bywater, which goes to the Industrial

Canal.* The Bywater is also known as the Upper Ninth Ward, as it is upstream from the Lower Ninth Ward, the section of the city between the Industrial Canal and St. Bernard Parish. The portion of Faubourg Marigny closest to the river was built up first; the area on the lake side of St. Claude Avenue (formerly Good Children Street) was sometimes called New Marigny. In the early nineteenth century, New Marigny was where white Creole gentlemen set up households for their mistresses of color (and their offspring) in the tradition of *plaçage*. The Marigny is considered a more Bohemian-type of community these days (and the Bywater even more so), although gentrification is changing this.

There were four breweries in the Bywater area, all along the river and all short-lived. The first was that of John Gros, who built a small plant on the river at Independence and North Peters Streets in 1872. He lasted in business until 1874. His building is long gone now, the land having been subsumed into the levee structure.

In 1888, Albert Erath moved the Pelican Brewery operations from Villere Street to Chartres Street, between Louisa and Clouet Streets. In 1890, the business was merged into the New Orleans Brewing Association. In 1910, it closed. The site is on the river side of Chartres; today, it's a parking lot. About the same time as Pelican made its move, the Belgian Brewery was opened. It was located on Montegut Street near the Pelican Brewery, according to John Nau,[35] but I have found no trace of it on any maps of the period. I suspect that it was a contract brewery, using the Pelican facility to produce its beer.

The last brewery in the Bywater was the ill-fated Home Brewing Company, located on North Peters at Jeanne (now Alvar) Street in the Bywater. The brewery proper was built in the later half of 1892† and burned to the ground on June 1, 1893.[36] Like John Gros's brewery, the site is now part of the levee structure and not accessible to the public. On the other hand, this section of the *batture* (the land between the river and the levee proper) is being currently developed into a park, so this could change.

In the Marigny proper, there have been seven breweries over the years. The first was that of Joseph Christen, who moved to the Marigny from the French Quarter in 1857. This brewery was on Moreau Street (now Chartres) between Spain and Engein (sometimes spelled "Engine," now St.

---

* The Inner Harbor Navigation Canal—usually just called the Industrial Canal—did not exist at this time. It wasn't built until much later, opening in 1923.
† An ordinance (#6302, dated April 23, 1892) listed it as being there as a new business and granted permission to build and operate there.

The former site of Joseph Christen's (later Caspar Lusse's) brewery, now a private home. *Argyle Wolf-Knapp.*

Roch Avenue) Streets. Christen brewed until 1867; the facility sat vacant until 1870, when it was bought by Caspar Lusse, who ran the brewery (advertising it as "This Brewery, the *only one* in New Orleans" in an ad in 1872)[37] until his death in 1879. His son, Henry, ran it for another year before closing it down. The brewery was eventually demolished, and a barbershop was built on the site. The barbershop was later converted into a private home and has since been landmarked.

In 1866, Joseph Fabacher opened a small brewery at 529 Cascaval Street (now 2621 Royal). He was out of business in just under a year and returned to his family's hotel business at 137 Royal Street in the French Quarter. The brewery building itself is no longer there. As with Lusse's brewery, the site is currently occupied by a private home.

In 1867, Jacob Armbruster opened his Orleans Brewery at 537 (now 2837) Chartres Street, on the downtown lakeside corner of Chartres and St. Ferdinand Streets, across Chartres from the New Orleans Center for Creative Arts. (The NOCCA building was the Crescent City jute mill; the architectural resemblance to New England fiber mills is unmistakable.) Armbruster went out of business in 1887. The site is currently occupied by artists' studios.

In 1870, Sebastian Soulé moved his business to 112–14 (now 2707–09) North Peters Street, on the corner of Port Street. His head brewer was

Henry Lusse, whose father, Caspar, had bought Joseph Christen's brewery in 1869. Soulé went out of business in 1891, although his bottling works (on the Decatur Street side of the block) continued operations as the World Bottling Company. World Bottling introduced a full line of other soft drinks (including an almond soda called Dr. Nut); it was eventually bought by the Wright Root Beer Company of Baton Rouge. For a time, the site was a warehouse for a storage and transfer company. Today, a roasting plant for PJ's Coffee is located there.

In 1872, as John Gros was opening up a bit downriver, Ernest Volkmann opened his Star Steam Brewery at 11–13 St. Ferdinand Street (now 425—essentially a loading dock). As with Gros, he was out of business by 1875.

On June 22, 1899, Charles Karst opened the Columbia Brewery on Chartres Street between Frenchmen Street and Elysian Fields Avenue.[38] Over ten thousand people showed up for the opening festivities. Columbia's beer was promptly acclaimed as one of the best in New Orleans, and the company produced 180 barrels a day when it opened. When Prohibition came, it tried to survive by making soft drinks (notably Omar Root Beer, "aged in wood, served in bottles only"),[39] but by 1924 it was bankrupt. In 1927, the building was exchanged for a home in Chicago. Most of the building is gone today; two-thirds of the site is a parking lot, and the rest is occupied by a shotgun double house/café, two restaurants and Café Brasil.

In 1919, the Union Brewery moved its operations from its Decatur Street location to a new fireproof, four-story facility at 2809–29 North Robertson Street at Press Street. It produced Union Beer and Old Union Ale and enjoyed a good reputation. It also made soft drinks to get through Prohibition, doing business as the Union Beverage Company and later as Union Products Company, Inc. While it survived Prohibition, it couldn't survive consolidation-era competition. Union closed in 1939 and sold the brand names and recipes to the Louisiana Brewery, which produced them until 1943. The building sat vacant for several years; after Hurricane Betsy, it was purchased by the Schneider Paper Products Company. Schneider renovated the building and operated there until 2005, when Hurricane Katrina shut down the city. The Schneider Company has since relocated to Baton Rouge. The brewery was sold in 2011 to a developer, who is converting it into artists' lofts.

LOWER CENTRAL BUSINESS DISTRICT AND ALGIERS

Bernard Xavier Philippe de Marigny de Mandeville, for all of his name and prestige, was indirectly responsible for the early development of the CBD and Uptown areas of New Orleans. While he owned the Marigny District pretty much outright, he hated the English people and anyone who spoke the language and refused to sell or lease property to them. Thus, English speakers were obliged to get land upriver from the French Quarter and take their business there. The upshot of this was to create an English-speaking zone just upriver, which became an economic powerhouse known as the city of Lafayette. In 1850, this was annexed by New Orleans.[40] Algiers, on the West Bank of the Mississippi River, was annexed in 1870.

About the same time as George Guth was opening his Louisiana Brewery on Conti Street, Jacob Zoelly opened his City Brewery on Delord (now Howard) Street, between Camp and Magazine Streets. The brewery proper was at the corner of Magazine, the Camp Street end being used for stables and a wagon yard. Zoelly's operation was quite a bit larger than Guth's and lasted a bit longer as well, until 1868. On April 20, 1873, Joseph Conrad Meyers bought the Camp Street end of the property for $5,000 at a sheriff's sale and went on to build several houses on the lot. On August 12 of that same year, the Magazine Street portion was sold to Jean Joseph Weckerling for $28,000. Weckerling had made a fortune in the shoe business and decided to try brewing—and did very well by it. He initially named his brewery the Louisiana Brewing Company. In 1875, he shortened it to the Louisiana Brewery—that name having been unused since 1861. He built and opened a second branch in 1885 on Jackson Avenue at Tchoupitoulas (previously the site of the Crescent City Railroad depot) and closed the Magazine Street location in order to build a much larger facility there.

The new building was designed by William Fitzner (who also designed the Louisiana, Lafayette and Standard Breweries).[41] On October 13, 1888, Weckerling opened this huge, brand-new brewery[42] and named it after himself. Two years later, he merged it into the New Orleans Brewing Association in conjunction with the Louisiana, Southern, Lafayette, Pelican and Crescent Breweries. It was in operation until Prohibition but closed down rather than try to get by making soft drinks. In 1925, the building was sold to the Gallagher Transfer and Storage Company, and in 1995 it was sold again to eventually become the home of the National D-Day Museum (now the National World War II Museum) in June 2000.

Weckerling himself never saw the ravages of Prohibition; he sold his interest in the brewery to Peter Blaise in 1902 and died in 1908.

A year after Guth and Zoelly opened their breweries, the Swiss-born Louis Fasnacht opened his, along with his brother Samuel. The Fasnacht Brewery was located at the intersection of Annunciation and Poeyferre Streets and included the old Poeyferre home.[43] It stayed in business until 1868, selling out to Eugene Erath & Co. Erath went out of business in 1871, whereupon Samuel Fasnacht bought back the brewery and tried to revive it. He gave it up in 1875. In 1882, the brewery and everything else on that block was bought by Arthur Maginnis, who proceeded to build the world's largest cotton mill there. In 1914, Maginnis was convicted of tax fraud, and the mill was sold. It was then broken up into smaller cotton job shops and continued in operation until the mid-1980s. It's currently a luxury apartment complex, the Cotton Mill Apartments.[44]

The year 1861 saw the opening and closing of the Massey Hutson Brewery at 52 New Levee (now 463 South Peters, part of what is now the W Hotel on Poydras Street). The hostilities and difficulties of the American Civil War probably had a deleterious effect on business; in any event, Massey Hutson didn't last. In total, only four New Orleans breweries survived the Civil War—those of Jacob Zoelly, Louis Fasnacht, Joseph Christen and George Merz.

Within a year of the war's end, four more breweries opened up, bringing the active total to eight. These were the Fred W. Boebinger Brewery, located at 215 (now 715) South Liberty Street;* the F. Weinmann Brewery at 130 (now 1350) Perdido Street;† the Joseph Fabacher Brewery at 529 Cascaval (now 2621 Royal) Street; and the Adam Heen Brewery in the town of Carrollton, located at "Fifth, c. of Jackson." (I'll deal with these last two in other sections.)

Weinmann's lasted only until 1867, Boebinger's until 1869. As Weinmann closed down, Sebastian Soulé opened his brewery at 114 Front Street (now 724 Convention Center Boulevard, a parking lot between Girod and Julia Streets). Soulé operated here for a bit under three years before moving operations to the Marigny.

---

* This is located just off what is now Champion's Square, on the river side of the street between Girod and Poydras at the base of Periliat Street. It can be found on a map at: http://www.notarialarchives.org/robinson/atlas/robinson4.html#.
† Like so many of the older breweries, no trace of the building remains. The site is part of the New Orleans City Hall campus, just riverward of the main stairs. See the same plate of the Robinson Atlas as Boebinger's.

Security Brewing logo. *Jeremy Labadie.*

In 1888, the short-lived People's Brewery opened operations at 35 (now 300) Carondelet Street, between Girod and Union. The building is gone. A branch of Capital One Bank is there now.

In 1892, Peter Blaise opened the Algiers Brewing Company at 4 Villere (later 104 Morgan) Street on Algiers Point shortly after closing the Hope Brewery. In early June 1893, it burned down.[45] Rebuilding proved impossible, and by 1894, the brewery was in receivership. The equipment was sold to the Columbia Brewing Company of St. Louis.[46] Blaise then opened the Security Brewing Company, apparently just transferring operations to central New Orleans under a new name and fresh funding. Security Brewing was located at 341–45 North Market Street (now North Diamond Street) and fronted on St. Joseph Street.[47] The building is still there, and the emblem of Security Brewing (a stylized eagle chained to a large *S*, holding barley and a threshing flail) can still be seen worked into the brickwork on the third-floor façade facing St. Joseph Street. It remained in operation until 1913.

In 1933, as Prohibition ended, a third People's Brewery was opened at 740 Perdido Street. It never got into commercial production and closed within the year.

In 1934, the short-lived Pelican Brewery (second to use the name but no connection to the original) opened at 810 Union Street, closing shortly thereafter.

In 2000, the Gordon Biersch brewpub chain of Palo Alto, California, opened a branch at 200 Poydras Street in the Harrah's Hotel.[48] It does a very strong business in sleek surroundings, offering five staple beers plus seasonal brews. In addition to the brewpubs of the chain, Biersch also brews more of its beers in a regular brewery for the market, so they're easy to get at a store.

BREWERIES OF UPTOWN NEW ORLEANS, INCLUDING THE CITY OF LAFAYETTE AND THE TOWN OF CARROLLTON

In 1860, brewing started in the Uptown section as well, with Nicholas Schmidt opening his brewery on Philip Street, near Annunciation in the recently annexed city of Lafayette.[49] Unfortunately for him, he was out of business by the end of 1861. I think the war might have had something to do with it.

In 1866, just after the war ended, Adam Heen opened a brewery in the town of Carrollton, located at "Fifth, c. of Jackson."[50] The town of Carrollton had several streets that had the same names as other streets in New Orleans. After Carrollton was annexed in 1874, over one-third of the streets in Carrollton were renamed to eliminate this duplication. Fifth Street was renamed Poplar in 1894 and, in 1924, again renamed Willow (tying it into the rest of the Uptown New Orleans grid). Jackson was renamed General Ogden in 1894.[51] On the *Robinson Atlas* of 1884, there is only one building shown at that intersection. I suspect, but cannot prove, that this was Heen's brewery (and probably his home as well). Adam Heen was registered as operating a brewery in 1866. I have no record of anything earlier or later for him, although the town of Carrollton census lists him as a brewer at this address from 1851 until 1874.

A year later, in 1867, Henry Bassemeir opened the Lafayette Brewery at 1010 (now 3110) Tchoupitoulas at Ninth Street with Nicholas Gunther. The brewery was a three-story building and took six months and $30,000 to build. In 1890, he merged the Lafayette Brewery with the New Orleans Brewing Association, which promptly closed the plant in 1892. It was eventually demolished as part of the development of the Port of New Orleans. The site is now part of the rail and truck roadway of the port next to the Seventh Street wharf and mostly hidden behind the flood wall.

In 1869, George Auer opened his Coffeehouse & Brewery at 540 (now 1640) Tchoupitoulas Street, between Market and St. James Streets. In 1870, he renamed it the Eagle Brewery and produced Eagle Beer ("It soars above all")[52] and Double Eagle Ale until 1887. The Eagle site is currently occupied

The former site of Lafayette Brewing. *Argyle Wolf-Knapp.*

The former site of George Auer's Eagle Brewery, now the site of an electrical transfer station. *Argyle Wolf-Knapp.*

by a 230 kV electrical step-down station. To see it now, you'd never guess that a brewery had been there.

In 1885, J.J. Weckerling opened a second branch of his Louisiana Brewing Company on the block bordered by Jackson Avenue, Tchoupitoulas, Philip and Rousseau Streets. This had previously been the site of the Crescent City Railroad depot. In 1890, it merged into the New Orleans Brewing Association and was renamed the Louisiana Branch of NOBA. Several beers were produced here over the years, including 4-X Beer (1933–49), Union Beer and Old Union Ale (1939–43) and Eagle Beer and Double Eagle Ale (1937–44). It went out of business in 1949. The main building is still standing and is part of a marine repair works. The bottling plant (on the uptown corner of Tchoupitoulas and Jackson) was demolished; that lot remains empty to this day.

Post-Katrina, there were no active breweries left in New Orleans, besides the two brewpubs downtown. In 2008, Kirk Coco, a local home brewer, and Peter Caddoo, a former brewer for Dixie, decided to change this by opening New Orleans' only (for now, anyway) true brewery. Their NOLA Brewing Company[53] is located in a pair of World War II–era aircraft repair hangars on the uptown corner of Seventh and Tchoupitoulas Streets, just two blocks from where Henry Bassemier had his Lafayette Brewery in the late 1800s. NOLA is a brewery, not a brewpub, and until recently could not sell its beers directly to anyone but a distributor. Louisiana has recently changed the laws concerning that, and NOLA's new tap room is open to the public Mondays, Wednesdays, Thursdays and Fridays from 2:00 p.m. until 11:00 p.m. and from 11:00 a.m. to 11:30 p.m. on Saturdays and Sundays. It produces four staple beers and five seasonal ones and does many experimental brews as well (the recent Mechahopzilla comes to mind—a huge beer; I think it should be classified as a double-Imperial India Pale Ale). NOLA also gives free tours of the brewery most Friday afternoons beginning at 11:45 a.m. Its future looks great.

BREWERIES OF MID-CITY

Mid-City New Orleans is not the same as the Central Business District. It's a newer section of the city, centered on the intersection of Canal Street and Carrollton Avenue. (The Central Business District is on the river from Canal Street to the I-90 Bridge.)

Peter Blaise's City Brewery at 180 (now 536) Perdido Street was the first brewery to open in Mid-City. It opened in 1869 and was Blaise's first foray in the industry—although far from his last. The City Brewery was renamed the Hope Brewery in 1873 and continued in operation until 1891. It was located on what is now part of the LSU Hospital complex on South Prieur Street.

In 1898, Peter Blaise opened another brewery: the Standard Brewing Company, which expanded the former Hope Brewery site by a factor of four. His partners were Henry Bassemeir (whose Lafayette Brewery had closed in 1892 after merging with the New Orleans Brewing Association) and Charles Wirth. The plant was seven stories tall and cost $100,000 to build, and the contract exempted the builder from any late penalties should there be an outbreak of yellow fever. Given that the penalties were steep and the last outbreak had happened in 1878, this seems to have been an eminently fair arrangement. Standard made Wirthbru "Weigelstyle" Beer, among others, and remained independent until 1947, when it was purchased by the American Brewing Company. Despite American's best efforts, the plant was shuttered in 1951. The site is currently occupied by part of the LSU Hospital complex. Peter Blaise died in 1910, leaving behind a legacy of which most of us can only be envious.

During the malaria outbreak of 1905, the Consumer's Brewing Company opened on South Liberty Street between Clio and Calliope Streets. It lasted in business until 1924, another victim of Prohibition. The site is currently vacant—and oddly difficult to get to.

The shell of the Dixie Brewing building. *Argyle Wolf-Knapp.*

Dixie Brewing, 2013. *Jeremy Labadie.*

George Merz's nephew[54] Valentine Merz opened the Dixie Brewery in 1907.[55*] In 1899, he had been elected president of the New Orleans Brewing

---

* He had worked with his uncle at the Old Canal Brewery and eventually became a mover and shaker in the brewing industry in his own right. He took over the Blatz beer distribution in New Orleans and eventually did the same for Anheuser-Busch. In 1884, he bought a saloon from Jules Krust and ran it until 1898, selling it to Charles Kolb in order to become the first president of the Dixie Brewing Company.

THE BEST BOTTLE BEERS UNDER THE FLAG

THE NATIONAL
BREWING CO.'S

EAGLE BREW AND OLD HEIDELBERG

A National Brewing Company advertisement. *From the* Herald, *March 16, 1916, page 2, image 2, volume XXIII, issue 45. Louisiana State University Library via Chronicling America, Library of Congress.*

Association and in 1906 was appointed president of Dixie, while the brewery was being built.[56] The Dixie strategy for success in brewing was to create diversity in branding and thus obtain more market share. Its motto—"One Brewery, 45 Brands"—was emblazoned on its trucks[57] and billboards, and this marketing scheme worked like a charm. Dixie dealt with Prohibition by making malt extract and powder, as well as creating a soft-drink line. After repeal, it brewed specialty beers for various local stores in addition to its flagship brew. In 1985, the brewery was bought by Joe and Kendra Bruno, who own it today. What stopped Dixie was Hurricane Katrina and the looting that followed. The brewery building itself has since been condemned to make way for the new LSU Mid-City medical complex. Currently, Dixie is being brewed under contract by the Minhas Craft Brewery in Monroe, Wisconsin, although there are longer-range plans to bring it back to New Orleans[58] in the not-too-distant future.

In 1911, National Brewing opened operations at the intersection of Gravier and South Dorgenois Streets. It resurrected Eagle Beer and Ale (previously made by George Auer) and eventually also began producing Falstaff Beer under contract from the Lemp Brewing Company of St. Louis. During Prohibition, it was renamed the National Beverage Company and produced a line of soft drinks in addition to nonalcoholic malt beverages. In 1937, Falstaff bought the business outright, installed a statue of King Gambrinus and put up a weather-forecasting tower. It also stopped producing Eagle Beer, although it dealt the name rights and recipe to the Louisiana Brewery, which produced Eagle until 1944.

Falstaff Brewery.

King Gambrinus still holds court over New Orleans beer drinkers.
Jeremy Labadie.

Falstaff stayed in production until 1979; the building then sat abandoned until after Hurricane Katrina. Since then, the brewery building has been converted into an apartment complex, the weather tower has been restored and King Gambrinus still watches over it all.

No other breweries opened in Mid-City until 1996, when Doug Lindley opened his Acadian Brewing Company and Beer Garden[59] at 201 North Carrollton Avenue. It lasted until 2002. A branch office of Gulf Coast Bank is there now.

A CONCISE TIME LINE OF NEW ORLEANS BREWERY EVENTS, 1726–PRESENT, WITH OTHER EVENTS

1726   Brasserie opens

1845   Stadtsbreuerei opens

1851   Louisiana and City Breweries open

1852   Fasnacht & Brand Brewery opens

1853   Cholera and yellow fever outbreaks

1854   Joseph Christen Brewery opens in Vieux Carré

1857   Christen Brewery moves to Moreau Street; Gottwald Brewery opens

1858   George Merz opens Coffeehouse & Brewery

1860   Gottwald Brewery closes; Karl Krost and Nicholas Schmidt open their respective breweries

1861   Outbreak of Civil War

1862   New Orleans captured by Union forces; Louisiana, Krost and Schmidt Breweries close

1865   Civil War ends

1866   George Merz renames his brewery the Old Canal Brewery; Fred Boebinger, F. Weinmann, Joseph Fabacher and Adam Heen open their breweries

1867   Fabacher closes, as does Heen; Jacob Armbruster (Orleans) opens, as do Sebastian Soulé and Henry Bassemier (Lafayette)

1868   City Brewery moves to Magazine and Delord; Christen Brewery closes

1869   Marais Street Steam, Hope and George Auer all open; Fasnacht is sold to Eugene Erath; Merz installs artificial refrigeration equipment

1870   City Brewery closes; Caspar Lusse opens in former Christen Brewery; Pelican opens

1872   Samuel Fasnacht buys brewery back from Eugene Erath; John Gros and Ernest Volkmann open their breweries

1873   J.J. Weckerling buys City Brewery and reopens it as Louisiana Brewery

1874   Gros and Volkmann close

1875   Fasnacht goes out of business again

1878   Yellow fever outbreak; Old Canal Brewery closes

1880   Caspar Lusse dies; his son, Henry, takes over

1881   Lusse closes

1882   Southern opens on expanded Old Canal site

1885   Louisiana Brewery opens a second branch on Jackson
        Avenue; Weckerling begins construction of a new, much
        larger facility on the original Delord Street site

1886   Marais Street Steam closes

1887   Crescent opens; Orleans and Soulé close

1888   Weckerling opens a new brewery on the original site; Pelican
        moves to Bywater site; People's opens

1890   New Orleans Brewing Association forms with six breweries:
        Weckerling, Southern, Crescent, Pelican, Lafayette and
        Louisiana; Jackson opens; People's closes

1891   American opens

1892   Hope and Crescent close; Algiers opens

1893   Lafayette and Soulé close; Home opens and promptly burns
        down on June 1; Algiers closes

1894   Security opens; Algiers is sold to Columbia Brewing Co.

1898   Standard opens on expanded Hope site

1899   Columbia opens

1901   Southern closes

1905   Malaria outbreak; Consumer's opens

1907   Dixie opens

1908   People's CO-OP opens

1910   People's CO-OP closes

1911   Pelican closes; Union and National open

1912   First delivery of beer to New Orleans by air

1914   Security closes; outbreak of World War I

1915   Hurricane

1918   Spanish flu

1920   Prohibition enacted; Weckerling closes

1922	National changes its name to National Beverage Co. and produces soft drinks, as do Dixie, Union, Standard, American, Jackson, Louisiana and Consumer's
1924	Columbia and Consumer's close
1933	Prohibition ends
1936	National is bought by Falstaff
1938	Outbreak of World War II
1939	Union closes
1945	World War II ends
1947	Hurricane
1948	American buys Standard
1950	Louisiana closes
1952	American closes Standard
1956	Jackson acquires the name Jax from the Jax Brewery of Jacksonville, Florida
1959	Vietnam War begins
1963	American closes
1965	Hurricane Betsy
1969	Hurricane Camille
1974	Jax closes
1979	Falstaff closes
1991	Crescent City Brewhouse opens
1996	Acadian Brewery & Beer Garden opens
1998	Hurricane Georges
2000	Gordon Biersch brewpub opens
2002	Acadian closes
2004	Hurricane Ivan
2005	Hurricanes Katrina and Rita; Dixie closes local operations
2008	Hurricane Gustav; NOLA opens
2012	Hurricane Isaac

CHAPTER 3
THE CRAFT BREWING MOVEMENT IN LOUISIANA

Jack McAuliffe opened the first craft brewery in America post-Prohibition in October 1976: the New Albion Brewing Company of Sonoma, California. This caused quite a stir in the brewing world, and the (then-underground) American Homebrewers' Association ramped up lobbying efforts to make its hobby legal again. After much ado, home brewing was re-legalized in 1978[60] (a mere forty-five years after Prohibition ended), and the craft beer movement in America began to take off.* Jack McAuliffe ran into the same problems every brewery faces, and after six years of not making a profit, he packed it in. But the craft brew spark had caught, and a lot of home brewers all over the country had the same thought: "Hey, maybe I can do this full time!" The craft beer revolution had begun.

In 1986, just four years after New Albion closed its doors, the Abita Brewing Company[61] started in Abita Springs, Louisiana. That made two breweries operating in Louisiana, the other being Dixie. To say that Abita has thrived would be a gross understatement. It has grown into a regional powerhouse, distributing its beer nationally. One of its practices is selling a portion of its beer to benefit good causes. Fleur de Lis Restoration Pale Ale after Hurricane Katrina and, more recently, Save Our Shores Pilsner (to benefit local wetlands restoration) are only two of these projects.

---

* Some states held out longer than others on this. Alabama and Mississippi didn't legalize it until 2013.

#DrinkLocal. *Jeremy Labadie.*

In 1999, the Day family opened the doors to Day Brewing Company, located at 5200 Taravella Road in Marrero, Louisiana, on the Westbank. This was the first Craft Brewery to operate in Jefferson Parish. The style of beer brewed was a Munich Helles German-style lager. It was brewed on a custom-built twenty-bbl brew house designed by brew master and owner Bernard (Sonny) Day. The brewery had an annual capacity of five thousand bbls. Day's beer was distributed in bottles and kegs throughout southern Louisiana. It was a casualty of Katrina and larger, related economics.

In 2005, Henryk "Heiner" Orlik opened the Heinerbrau Brewery in Covington, Louisiana, a bit south and west of Abita. Its flagship Kolsch did well, and it also produced the house beers for Zea, a local craft-beer restaurant chain. Orlik sold his interest in 2005, and the company has been renamed the Covington Brewhouse.[62] It has expanded the number of beers it makes, although keeping to German styles as a rule.

On St. Patrick's Day 2009, the Bayou Teche Biere[63] Company was opened in Arnaudville. It is focused on making beers to go with Cajun food and experiments with all sorts of ingredients.

The boys from Bayou Teche Brewing jam out with some authentic Cajun music. *Jeremy Labadie.*

November 2010 saw the Tin Roof Brewing Company[64] of Baton Rouge enter the market. It cans all of its beers rather than bottling them (as does NOLA), which makes them street-legal for New Orleans!

In 2011, the Chafuncta Brewing Company[65] opened in Mandeville, just across Lake Pontchartrain from New Orleans, a tad south of Covington. So did the Parish Brewing Company[66] in Broussard. Parish's Canebrake wheat beer made an instant impact on the local market, being the first to use Steen's cane syrup in the mix—not unlike using molasses in the manufacture of city beer back in the 1850s.

There are several other Louisiana breweries in the works at the moment: 40 Arpent[67] in Arabi (just downriver from New Orleans), Gnarly Barley Brewing[68] in Hammond, the Mudbug Brewery[69] in Thibodaux, Great Raft Brewing in Shreveport[70] and two more in New Orleans itself: the Courtyard Brewery on Erato Street in the Lower Garden District and Cajun Fire Brewing[71] in New Orleans East. And to be fair, even Mississippi is getting in on this. Lazy Magnolia Brewing[72] in Kiln, Mississippi, should

Zac and Cari Caramonta from Gnarly Barley Brewing. *Gnarly Barley Brewing.*

certainly count as being in the same region as the rest listed here, even though it's not in Louisiana proper. Also, the Louisiana Tourism Board has recently created a "Louisiana Beer Trail" with an attendant website[73] listing and reviewing all seven currently operating Louisiana breweries, with maps to help get to each. And if all that isn't enough, the Louisiana Craft Beer Facebook page[74] is up and getting lively. Looks like brewing boom times are here again—and not a moment too soon!

SUPPORTIN' DAT LOCAL BEER

Abita Brewing Co.
21084 Louisiana 36
Covington, LA 70420
(985) 893-3143
http://abita.com
@TheAbitaBeer

Bayou Teche Brewing
1106 Bushville Highway,
Arnaudville, LA 70512
Phone:(337) 303-8000
http://bayoutechebrewing.com
@BayouTecheBiere

Chafunkta Brewing Company
21449 Marion Lane, Suite 2
Mandeville, LA 70471
985-869-2349
http://www.chafunktabrew.com
@ChafunktaBrew

Covington Brewhouse
226 East Lockwood Street,
Covington, LA 70433
Phone:(985) 893-2884
http://www.covingtonbrewhouse.com
@CovingtonBrew

Crescent City Brewhouse
527 Decatur Street,
New Orleans, LA 70130
(504) 522-0571
http://www.crescentcitybrewhouse.com
@crescentbrew

Gordon Biersch
200 Poydras Street,
New Orleans, LA 70130
Phone:(504) 552-2739
http://www.gordonbiersch.com
@Gordon_Biersch

Great Raft Brewing
1251 Dalzell Street,
Shreveport, LA 71104
(318) 734-8101

http://www.greatraftbrewing.com
@GreatRaftBeer

New Orleans Lager and Ale Brewing Company

3001 Tchoupitoulas Street,
New Orleans, LA 70115
(504) 896-9996
http://www.nolabrewing.com
@NOLABrewing

Old Rail Brewing Company

639 Girod Street,
Mandeville, LA 70448
(985) 612-1828
http://www.oldrailbrewery.com
@OldRailBeer

Parish Brewing Company

229 Jared Drive,
Broussard, LA 70518
(337) 330-8601
http://www.parishbeer.com
@ParishBrewing

Red River Brewing Company

1010 Marshall Street
Shreveport, LA 71101
(318) 464-1024
http://www.redriverbeer.com
@redriverbeer

Tin Roof Brewery

1624 Wyoming Street,
Baton Rouge, LA 70802
(225) 377-7022
http://www.tinroofbeer.com
@TinRoofBeer

Coming Soon!

40 Arpent Brewing
Bombastic Beers
Cajun Fire Brewing
Courtyard Brewing
George's Brewing
Gnarley Barley Brewing
Mudbug Brewing
Tu Lu Lu Brewery

HOME BREWING IN THE CRESCENT CITY

Brewing beer in general has a seven-thousand-year history beginning with the Egyptians and Sumarians. Once they figured out the whole agriculture thing, they figured out fermented beverages as well, and life has never been the same since. You know it's serious when you have a goddess devoted to brewing. That would be the Sumarians' Ninkasi.

Here in America, brewing beer has also been pretty important. Not have-a-god-of-brewing important, but still pretty important. We know the Native Americans brewed using maize and pumpkin, and the English colonists were most certainly brewing using the same ingredients, having learned from the locals. It's pretty awesome that our first president, George Washington, was an accomplished home brewer and apparently brewed a damn fine porter.

In Louisiana, home brewing became legal the same time President Carter signed bill HR 1337. This bill repealed federal restrictions and excise taxes on home brew. To be honest, I'm pretty sure home brewing never ceased because of laws. This *is* Louisiana, after all. We have a passionate group of home brewers here in Louisiana, and they are pumping out some amazing beers.

If you are interested in beginning home brewing, the following suppliers and clubs may be of interest.

Homebrew Shops

Brewstock
3800 Dryades Street
New Orleans, LA 70115
(504) 208-2788

Main Grain
70271 Louisiana 59
Abita Springs, LA 70420
(985) 674-5862

Homebrew Clubs

Bicycle Brew Club (Baton Rouge, LA), http://www.bicyclebrewclub.
   com/home
Brasseurs a la Maison (Baton Rouge, LA), http://www.brbrewers.
   com/default.cfm
Crescent City Homebrewers (New Orleans, LA), http://www.
   crescentcityhomebrewers.org
Dead Yeast Society (Lafayette, LA), http://www.deadyeast.com
Malt Munching Mash Monsters (Shreveport/Bossier City, LA),
   http://www.maltmunchingmashmonsters.com
Mystic Krewe of Brew (Northshore, LA), http://www.mkob.com
Redstick Brewmasters (Baton Rogue) http://www.redstickbrew
   masters.com
Shade Tree Brewers (Central Louisiana), no website

A Brief History of the Crescent City Home Brewers

By Carol Rice, ad hoc historian

Crescent City Homebrewers (CCH) is the oldest brew club in New Orleans, possibly in the whole Gulf region. After five years of very informal existence, members incorporated CCH with the state of Louisiana in 1983. The purpose of the club as stated in the bylaws of the corporation "shall be a non-profit, informational organization to promote brewing of beers in the home for personal consumption as an alternative to commercial brews."

The country's bicentennial in 1976 spurred a resurgence of interest in all colonial home crafts resulting in federal recognition of the craft of home brewing. In 1978, President Jimmy Carter signed a bill into law that made home brewing legal and exempt from excise tax but still subject to state local options in October. The law went

Grant Capone working on some home brew. *Jeremy Labadie.*

into effect four months later. Eight guys curious about making beer decided to give it a try.

The intrepid eight began with Fleischman's Yeast and Blue Ribbon Malt Extract from the A&P. They bought hops pellets (a delicate light brown color) from the home brew shop on Oleander Street, where the club met. "We started buying mail order because his stuff was not the freshest," generously stated Harold Hochhalter, 1985 CCH president. Until then, "we didn't know hops were supposed to be green," said John Dauenhauer, 1984 president. "The first recipes we had included three pounds of corn sugar per batch. Lots of alcohol but very little flavor," said Harold.

They were fearless. They tried everything, ales and lagers. Rumor has it that the club's first lagers were aged in the cooler of a funeral home where one of the members worked. Too bad the name of that beer was lost–*Laid Out Lager*, perhaps. Eventually, they tried all-grain brewing.

Club members built equipment large enough to brew fifty gallons at a time. Each guy would take a share home to ferment. They called it a Brew-Off. Club brews are still called that today. The equipment has been upgraded several times, but the result is still the same. Ten brewers go home with five gallons of wort to ferment and finish. CCH may be the only club in the country to brew in large cooperative batches. No other club in Louisiana does, nor in the other Gulf states.

CCH has also partnered with craft breweries to do even larger Brew-Offs with Mystic Krewe of Brew (MKOB), the North Shore club. Zea Rotisserie and Brewery, Big Easy Beer and Heiner Brau (now Covington Brew House) have all hosted joint Brew-Offs. The club uses Brew-Offs to introduce new brewers to all-grain brewing. Educating brewers in all-grain brewing is part of our mission statement. CCH has a continuous history of educating members about all aspects of beer. This began as a series of short articles in the *Hopline*, the monthly newsletter that began, sporadically, shortly after the club was formed. The *Hopline* was typed by the club president, mimeographed and mailed to the membership. It was quite entertaining, with crossword puzzles, Brew-Off recipes, topical jokes and quotes and social notes. Considering the technology, which now seems soooo primitive, the *Hopline* was quite an accomplishment. They were exuberant testaments to the joys and camaraderie of beer and brewing. It was not typeset until 1988, probably on an early personal computer.

The short technical *Hopline* articles about beer morphed over time into yearlong beer appreciation courses that cover beer-making procedures from shopping to finishing; storing and serving; the sciences involved; history; styles (usually following the BJCP style guidelines); tasting and evaluating; and preparing for judging. Warren Chigoy, the first instructor, taught the course for years. He has been followed by one of his students, Carol Rice. Both are BJCP certified.

CCH grew significantly over the years. By the early '90s, membership had reached 150 and included several women. The first woman documented as a member was Kathryn O'Brian, who joined in November 1986. The following June, Kendra Bruno, owner of Dixie Brewery, joined the club. The first female officer was Marci Kraus, club secretary in '88 and '89.

Club members held internal competitions right from the start but were thirsting for more feedback than their friends would give. So they went public. In 1991, CCH hosted its first invitational competition, the Crescent City Coast to Coast Competition (CCCCC). Invitations were sent nationwide. It grew to be an impressive event. New Orleans mayor Marc Morial applauded the effort. "The Crescent City Competition for '95 has so many events, the visitors might want to come a day early and stay a day after so they can really see…New Orleans." (January 1995 Crescent City Competition brochure) This competition settled down simply as the Crescent City Competition, part of the now-defunct Gulf Coast Series of Homebrew Competitions. Clubs from four cities in the Gulf region hosted four competitions that were amalgamated to name the Gulf Coast Home Brew Club of the Year and the Gulf Coast Home Brewer of the Year. They were: Crescent City Competition in New Orleans, hosted by CCH; Bluebonnet Brew-Off in Dallas, hosted by several clubs, including the North Texas Home Brewers Association

Dixie Brewing neon on the building. *Jeremy Labadie.*

Falstaff Brewing's weather tower still forecasts the weather. *Jeremy Labadie.*

Above: NOLA
Brewing taproom.
Jeremy Labadie.

Right: A Bayou Teche
cask at New Orleans
International Beer
Festival. *Jeremy Labadie.*

David Blossman of Abita Brewing explaining the anatomy of a hop. *Jeremy Labadie.*

Regal Brewing's logo on the side of Elizabeth's Restaurant. *Jeremy Labadie.*

The Falstaff logo painted on what was once a store but is now a house in the Bywater. *Jeremy Labadie.*

Another successful New Orleans beer share event. *Jeremy Labadie.*

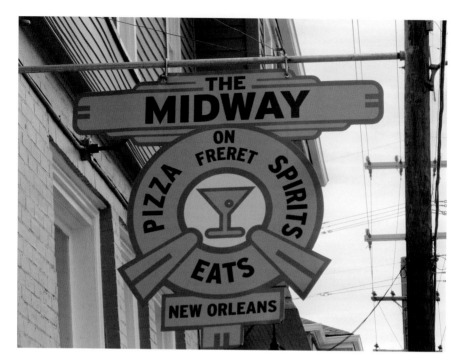

Midway Pizza on Freret Street. *Jeremy Labadie.*

Whiskey barrels with some Bayou Teche Miel Sauvage. *Aaron Labadie.*

Tap handles at Abita Brewing's Visitors' Center. *Jeremy Labadie.*

Snake and Jakes. *Jeremy Labadie.*

Painted Dixie Brewing logo on a building. *Wikimedia commons user Infrogmation.*

An old gas station with Regal and Jax signs, June 1940. *Marion Post Wolcott. Library of Congress, Prints & Photographs Division, FSA/OWI Collection, LC-DIG-fsac-1a34361.*

Jax Brewing building. *Wikimedia commons user Infrogmation.*

NOLA Brewing tanks. *Wikimedia commons user Infrogmation.*

Gnarly Barley Catahoula Common. *Courtesy Gnarly Barley Brewing.*

Gnarly Barley logo. *Courtesy Gnarly Barley Brewing.*

An old Jax Brewing can. *Jeremy Labadie.*

Parish Brewing's Dr. Hoptigon on the shelf at Stein's. *Jeremy Labadie.*

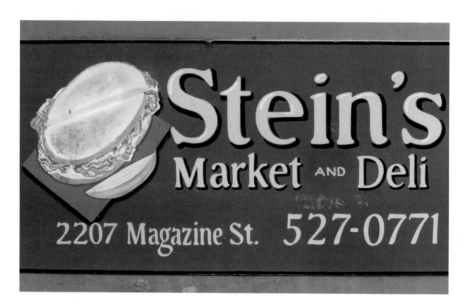

Stein's Deli. *Jeremy Labadie.*

The Bulldog, Magazine Street. *Jeremy Labadie.*

The Bulldog's tap fountain. *Jeremy Labadie.*

Breton Day from www.thealerunner.com enjoying some beer. *Jeremy Labadie.*

Zac (Gnarly Barley), Dylan (NOLA Brewing) and Josh (Chafunkta Brewing) hanging at the NOLA On Tap Beer Festival. *Gnarly Barly Brewing.*

Stein's Deli beer room. *Jeremy Labadie.*

This page and next: Zac from Gnarly Barley Brewing showing his brewing skills.

and Red River Brewers; Dixie Cup Homebrewing Competition in Houston, hosted by the Foam Rangers; and the Sunshine Challenge in Orlando, hosted by the Central Florida Home Brewers. The traveling trophy, the C-Cup, was designed (and "lovingly fashioned with his own hands" from a brassiere that size) by Louie Marino, a playful and talented member.

The rivalries to take the prize home were intense. Bert 'n' Ernie of CCH were always a challenge to the Sampsons of Central Florida Home Brewers. Unfortunately, the large competition became far too expensive for CCH to run alone. The club lost money every year. When no other Louisiana club would join in ("We aren't interested in losing money," said Jack Schugg, president of MKOB), CCH abandoned the Crescent City Competition in 2005. That was the death knell for the Gulf Coast Series of Home Brew Competitions.

Katrina had a serious effect on the club. Before Katrina, Carol Rice described the club as "a social club with closet brewers." Now, the club is full of serious (out-of-the-closet) brewers who make stunning beers and don't mind socializing with them one bit. The cadre of Tulane students in the club was washed away by the hurricane to graduate elsewhere. No Tulanians have joined since the storm. Too bad–they were a fun lot. Our meeting place, Deutsches Haus, was inundated and closed for more than a year. The club became a band of vagabonds, bouncing from place to place for meetings with mixed results. When Deutsches Haus reopened, CCH was very happy to return home. After a few rocky post-Katrina years, membership is back up to one hundred. The new members are as enthusiastic and energetic as the original intrepid eight. They think outside the box when building recipes. The days of being in lockstep with BJCP are long gone. The results are gorgeous, rich, sumptuous, unique and challenging brews. They are well worth the experimentation.

CCH is a good group of feet-on-the-ground people getting to enjoy a fun hobby with a fun product. They are all responsible drinkers. Our tag line says it all: For the responsible drinker, there is always another party.

Here's how the law reads:

United States Code of Federal Regulations, Title 27, Part 25, Subpart L, Section 25.205 and Section 25.206
Beer for Personal or Family Use
§ 25.205 Production.
(a) Any adult may produce beer, without payment of tax, for personal or family use and not for sale. An adult is any individual who is 18 years of age or older. If the locality in which the household is located requires a greater minimum age for the sale of beer to individuals, the adult shall be that age before commencing the production of beer. This exemption does not authorize the production of beer for use contrary to State or local law.
(b) The production of beer per household, without payment of tax, for personal or family use may not exceed:
(1) 200 gallons per calendar year if there are two or more adults residing in the household, or
(2) 100 gallons per calendar year if there is only one adult residing in the household.
(c) Partnerships except as provided in §25.207, corporations or associations may not produce beer, without payment of tax, for personal or family use.
§ 25.206 Removal of beer.
Beer made under §25.205 may be removed from the premises where made for personal or family use including use at organized affairs, exhibitions or competitions such as homemaker's contests, tastings or judging. Beer removed under this section may not be sold or offered for sale.

DISCUSSION
§ 205 provides an exemption to the code permitting the production of beer for personal or family use. § 206 allows for removal of beer from the home for

personal use as well as use at organized affairs and competitions. § 25.11 provides a definition for beer (see applicable statutory material). The Statute in Title 27, Part 25, Subpart L, Section 25.205 legalizing home production of beer, also appears in Title 26, Subtitle E, Chapter 51, Subchapter A, Part I, Subpart D, § 5053. The 1978 amendment to § 25.205 federally recognizing the home production of beer. Amendment XXI (1933) of the United States Constitution repealed the prohibition of intoxicating liquor (Amendment XVIII [1919]). However, section 2 of Amendment XXI and state police power gives states the authority to regulate the production, transportation and possession of intoxicating liquors. Therefore the home production of beer is recognized by federal statute so long as such production is not in violation of state law.

Beer Writers and Bloggers in the Big Easy

If you are looking for the newest beer news, most likely you are using the Internet to find those answers. And most likely you are going to get your answers from a beer blogger. Whether it is best beer bars, newest craft beer releases or newest brewery in town, your local beer blogger will generally have the best answers for you, and Louisiana is no exception. Below are the bloggers and professional writers who can help you with any questions you have about tasty suds in Louisiana.

Baton Rouge

Brenton Day, www.thealerunner.com
Eric Ducote, http://www.brbeerscene.com
Jay Ducote, http://www.biteandbooze.com

Houma

Dwayne Andras, http://theperfectpintofbeer.blogspot.com
Joel Ohmer, www.bayoubeersociety.com

Louisiana

Andy, http://thebeerinme.com
Tyler Cummings and Travis Sisson, http://drinkallthebeers.com

New Orleans

Matthew Austin, http://impouring.wordpress.com/about
Geoffrey Gauchet, http://slashbeer.net
Jeremy Labadie, www.thebeerbuddha.com
Nora McGunnigle, www.nolabeerblog.com
Todd Price, http://toddaprice.com

Enjoying some craft beer. *Jeremy Labadie.*

PART II

 THE GUIDES

CHAPTER 4

ALE AND BEER 101

A PRIMER TO THE GLORIOUS SUDS

A few words about beer in general are in order. Anyone who has brewed beer at home is familiar with the differences between ales and lager beers (or should be), but this is for the rest of us.

First off, it's all beer. Simply put, fermented fruit yields wine; fermented grains yield beer. Ales were the traditional style of English and Scandinavian beers and were the default Germanic beer type as well until the 1500s, when lagering was developed. Beer has been around since the Sumerians and early Egyptians were forces to be reckoned with. The oldest industrial facility ever discovered was an Egyptian brewery from roughly 6000 BC.[75]* Some of us believe that it was the discovery of beer that gave rise to agriculture—hunting and gathering doesn't cut it for brewing. Early beer was fermented with what we now refer to as ale yeast, a top-fermenting yeast that is ubiquitous to the planet. The earliest beers used dates and other fruits, as well as grains (sometimes baked into bread first),[76] and were sweet. They were carbonated, although not to the degree that modern beer is, and were less alcoholic as well.

Various herbal blends (generally referred to as *gruit*) have been used over the centuries to both flavor and stabilize beer, and throughout Europe and England, monasteries were granted a monopoly on both growing and selling

---

* The oldest continuously operating brewery in the world is Weihenstephan, in Freising, Germany, just northwest of Munich. It has operated under license since AD 1040 (twenty-six years before William the Bastard set out to conquer Great Britain and change his name).

gruit. Hops were known to be the most effective herb for stabilization and became common in Bavaria in the early medieval period. The first records we have of hops being cultivated come from the town of Hallertau in AD 736. The earliest documentation of them being used in brewing dates from AD 822. Their use gradually spread throughout Europe but only began to be used in England in the 1400s,[77] mostly due to Dutch influence during the draining of the Fenlands[78] area (although some English people objected to hops in their beer to the point of rioting on occasion as late as the mid-1500s).

Since grains are starchy (rather than sugary) things, in order to ferment them they must first be *malted*[79] and *mashed*.[80] In malting, grains are moistened and allowed to germinate in order to produce the enzymes (alpha amylase and beta amylase) necessary for mashing. The malted grains are then dried (and sometimes roasted to produce darker, richer flavors) in order to store them until the brewer is ready to use them. Brewing proper begins with the mashing. In mashing, the starches in the malted grains are converted to sugars by the actions of both amylase enzymes. Alpha amylase works at higher temperatures than beta amylase does and works by splitting starch molecules into smaller starch molecules and ultimately into sugars. This type of conversion yields a substantial amount of residual complex (non-fermentable) sugars. Beta amylase works by nibbling simple sugars from the ends of starch molecules. This type of conversion yields a very complete conversion of starches to simple, fermentable sugars. This difference in mashing technique is the primary source of the differences between traditional English and German styles of beer.

Traditional English ale brewing started with simply pouring boiling water over malted grains and covering it to rest overnight. This resulted in an almost exclusively alpha amylase conversion of starches because of the high initial heat of the process. The beer made from this *wort*[81] is lower in alcohol than the German style and retains some sweetness and a richer body. Typically, after drawing the wort off to be brewed, a second round of water then would be added to the mashed grains to make a second, thinner wort (the "second runnings"), which would then be fermented to make *small beer*.[82*] Small beer usually came in around 3 percent alcohol when brewed and was primarily used for household staff. It tastes like watery beer (or modern light beer, for that matter), which isn't surprising. A third runnings was sometimes done to produce a beverage called *switchel*,[83] which was given to field hands after

---

* Anchor Brewing in San Francisco makes a small beer from the mash used to make its Old Foghorn barley wine.

being flavored and sweetened a bit. (Modern barley water is the descendant of this and usually can be found where British food is sold.) The spent grains would then be composted or fed to cattle. Today, the mashed grains are usually rinsed ("sparged") after the initial wort is drawn off to extract all of the residual sugars into the initial wort rather than making small beer.

The German process[*] produces a primarily beta amylase conversion (both amylase types work until the temperature gets to 148 degrees Fahrenheit or so; the beta shuts down then) with very few complex sugars left. The majority of proteins are also broken down by this gradual process. The beer brewed from this mash ferments completely, yielding beer of higher alcohol and lighter body than the English style, as well as a liquid clearer to the eye.

Lager beers are not exactly ales. They are more like Ale 2.0—a more evolved form of beer. They are made with a species of yeast that ferments on the bottom of the wort rather than the top, as with ale yeast. Lager yeast is *Saccharomyces pastorianus* (also known as *Saccharomyces Carlsbergensis*) and was identified by Emil Christian Hansen in Denmark[84] in 1883.[†] It is actually a hybrid of ale yeast and a cold-loving Patagonian yeast that was brought to Europe in the early 1500s[85] and got loose.

What sets lager apart is the effect of extended fermentation and maturation. Indeed, the name *lager* comes from the Gothic *ligrs*, "place of lying down." Lager yeast works best in cool temperatures, and this long, cool fermentation produces flavors that ales simply cannot match.[86] As with wine, beer and ales also change with time. In the case of lager beer, this translates in the glass to a marked and highly desirable delicacy and complexity. The Pilsner style of beer, the highest form of lager, is thus the product of step-mashing, the use of lager yeast and the attendant cool aging for maturation. To really get what this means, have a Pilsener Urquell; the proof is in the glass.

Seasonal temperatures played a big part in the brewing calendar. If it got too hot, good beer could not be made. Thus, it was a seasonal occupation, starting in the fall and going through the spring. Summers were time off from brewing and the time for facility repair and expansion. In many ways, the brewer's year was the opposite of the farmer's. Of course, the lower the

---

* Usually referred to as "step-mashing," as the wort is repeatedly heated to specific temperatures and held there for a bit before being raised to the next point.
† The Carlsbergensis name was from an attempt by the Carlsberg Brewery to patent lager yeast as its own unique proprietary species of yeast, which would have meant a fortune in licensing fees. This attempt failed, fortunately.

latitude, the shorter the brewing season. The only way to get around this was to have cool places to work, which usually meant caves (natural or not). In Cincinnati, for instance, lagering tunnels were built in the 1800s,* some of which can be toured today.[87] Most are about forty feet below street level and maintain a steady temperature of about forty-eight degrees Fahrenheit year-round. Obviously, digging lagering tunnels is not a solution that would work in New Orleans. We had to wait for artificial refrigeration and keep everything at ground level or above.

---

* When the Christian Moerlein Brewery in Cincinnati was reopened in 1981, over fifteen thousand feet of lagering tunnels were uncovered under the brewery buildings. Amazingly enough, no one had known about them when the brewery was put back into operation!

CHAPTER 5

GREATER NEW ORLEANS BEER GUIDE

BYWATER/MARIGNY

(For book purposes, we combined the Bywater and Marigny; it just made geographic sense to do that.)

Beer is that important. *Jeremy Labadie.*

Pizza Delicious in the Bywater. *Jeremy Labadie.*

Pizza Delicious, 617 Piety Street, New Orleans, LA   70117

Pizza Delicious was started as a one-day-a-week pop-up pizza joint. When you're calling in six hours in advance to get a pizza, you know it must be good. It is now in a permanent location serving up amazing New York–style pizza with a fantastic craft beer selection as well, with Brooklyn and NOLA Brewing beers.

dba, 618 Frenchmen Street, New Orleans, LA   70117

dba has a huge, well-thought-out beer selection, but unlike its second location in New York City, this one also presents some great local music acts. While you're there, make sure you hoist a pint in honor of its founder, the late and much-lamented Ray Deter. It does not serve food, but you can bring in your own if you must.

Uptown/Garden District

Avenue Pub, 1732 St. Charles Avenue, New Orleans, LA 70130

The Avenue Pub is the place to go for the serious craft beer lover. Open twenty-four hours a day and with what many consider the best craft beer selection in town, you're always bound to find something you have not tried before. Check its website[88] for upcoming beer events; there's almost always something good going on in the way of release parties or commemorative events like Zwanze Day. It also offers a daily Crafty Hour (4:00 to 6:00 p.m., two dollars off all American craft beers) and Firkin Fridays (every Friday at 6:30 p.m., it taps a cask of Real Ale). You can drink downstairs or go upstairs and enjoy the balcony. Unlike dba, it also serves food. And it's open for Mardi Gras—with restrooms!

Avenue Pub is without a doubt one of the best craft beer bars in the state. *Jeremy Labadie.*

Stein's Deli, 2207 Magazine Street, New Orleans, LA 70130

This Jewish-style deli run by Philly transplant Dan Stein not only has amazing deli sandwiches such as the Rachel, the Phillie (an authentic Philly-style cheese steak) and the Fancy Schmancy Cuban, but it also has a back room with what many consider to be the best retail beer selection in town.

Above: Gnarly Barley bottle of brew. *Gnarly Barley Brewing.*

Right: Stein's Deli is your choice for retail craft beer and killer sandwiches. *Evangeline Labadie.*

Midway Pizza, 4725 Freret Street, New Orleans, LA 70115

Pizza and beer go hand-in-hand, and if you're looking for something different than a New York–style pie, Midway is your place. This is a deep-dish-style pizza, and the craft beer selection is awesome. The Money Pie is an amazing choice and goes well with almost any beer.

Squeal BBQ, 8400 Oak Street, New Orleans, LA 70118

Squeal BBQ on Oak Street is not your average barbecue joint. Think of this place as more of a restaurant than a joint. It will have your regular barbecue fare like pulled pork, ribs and beef brisket, but it likes to kick things up with barbecue tacos. Not much goes better with some barbecue than some great craft beer—and Squeal has it!

Squeal BBQ. *Jeremy Labadie.*

The Bulldog, 3236 Magazine Street, New Orleans, LA 70115

The Bulldog on Magazine Street is in a great location and tends to have a lot of college kids from Tulane and Loyola hanging around drinking beer. The beer selection is solid with quantity and quality, and there is a small patio with an amazing beer tap fountain. If you need to stock up on some shaker pints, head over there on Wednesday nights for its pint glass giveaway. And make sure you get the Crawfish Banditos—they go great with any beer.

Snake & Jake's Christmas Club Lounge, 7612 Oak Street, New Orleans, LA 70118

The dive bar that will outdo all other dive bars is without a doubt Snake & Jake's. This shack in the middle of an Uptown neighborhood is legendary amongst New Orleans beer drinkers. If you have not been, it's a must go. But for the love of God, stick to straight beer and liquor—a cocktail place this ain't!

Ms. Mae's The Club, 4336 Magazine Street, New Orleans, LA 70115

Ms. Mae's is a New Orleans bar institution. This twenty-four-hour dive is your cheap beer mecca, especially during Mardi Gras, as it sits right on the

Ms. Mae's on Magazine Street. *Jeremy Labadie.*

parade route. It recently raised its prices: a shot is now two dollars or three dollars for a double.

Whole Foods, 5600 Magazine Street, New Orleans, LA 70115

As far as grocery stores goes, Whole Foods locations are always a great place for craft beer—and the branch here in New Orleans is no exception. While picking up your craft beer, don't forget to pick up some artisanal bread and cheeses.

Breaux Mart, 3233 Magazine Street, New Orleans, LA 70115

This small, locally owned grocery store (located on Magazine Street right across from The Bulldog) has a nice diverse selection of craft beer and imports.

Elio's Wine Warehouse, 6205 South Miro Street, New Orleans, LA 70125

Elio's was founded in 1993 and serves what is known as the University Village section of Uptown. With its amazing beer selection, there's no excuse for Tulane and Loyola University kids to be drinking crappy beer. Elio's is also one of the top locations for kegged beer.

Cooter Brown's, 509 South Carrollton Avenue, New Orleans, LA 70118

Cooter Brown's is a legend in New Orleans. It has a nice beer selection on tap and a huge bottle selection. DO NOT go by its online beer list as it hasn't been updated in a long time. Cooter Brown's has beers on the list that aren't even distributed here. I would highly recommend the cheese fries, Radiator's Special and the NOLA Philly.

NOLA Brewing Company Tap Room, 3001 Tchoupitoulas Street, New Orleans, LA 70115

Louisiana came a bit more to its senses recently and decided that Louisiana craft breweries could sell up to 10 percent of their products directly to the public—just like brewpubs. A happy result is the NOLA Tap Room, where you can get not only all of its regular releases but most of the experimental ones as well! Its rum-cask-aged Hurricane Saison, for instance, was a small-batch experiment and thus not destined for distribution. The taproom gave the public a chance to experience it—with luck, it (and more than a few other brews) may make it to market. At least, I certainly hope so. There's no food offered here, nor any beers other than NOLA beers—not a problem! Open Wednesdays to Mondays from 11:00 a.m.

FRENCH QUARTER

Rouses, 701 Royal Street, New Orleans, LA 70116

This is a grocery store, but it has a great selection of beer. Stone, Bayou Teche, Abita, plus twenty-four-ounce cans of whatever cheap beer you might want. And remember: you CAN walk around the streets of New Orleans with open beer. It just needs to be in a non-glass container.

Jimani Lounge, 141 Chartres Street, New Orleans, LA 70130

Located at the corner of Chartres Street and Iberville, this French Quarter hole-in-the-wall has a great mix of low-priced brews and local craft like NOLA and Abita, as well as many other craft beers.

Jäger Haus, 833 Conti Street, New Orleans, LA 70112

An authentic German restaurant in the French Quarter? Yes. Their beer selection is ALL imports, but hey, it's a German restaurant. What do you expect? And you should have the Wiener schnitzel with an Ayinger Celebrator. It's delicious. And you get to say "wiener" when you order.

Crescent City Brewhouse, 527 Decatur Street, New Orleans, LA 70130

This is the oldest brewing establishment in New Orleans, started by Wolfram Koehler in 1991. It mostly serves its own beers (duh!) but also has a full bar and some bottled beers. It has four staple beers (Pilsner, Vienna Copper, Dark Munich and Weissebier), as well as seasonal offerings.

CBD/Warehouse District

Basically, this is the area with all the big buildings not in the French Quarter. There's not much going on in this area beer-wise, but here are my recommendations:

Gordon Biersch, 200 Poydras Street, New Orleans, LA 70130

If you're looking for a brewpub, this is one of only two in the city. Gordon Biersch is a chain restaurant, but the beer is brewed on premise by Tom Conklin, who won a silver medal at the Great American Beer Festival in 2009 for his Pilsner. The food is killer, and the beer pairs perfectly with all the meals.

Cochon Butcher, 930 Tchoupitoulas Street, New Orleans, LA 70130

Cochon Butcher is not only a butcher shop but also a sandwich shop, and man are the sandwiches amazing. It has a small but solid bottle list. I recommend the Cochon Muffaletta with the Bayou Teche LA 31 Biere Pale.

Capdeville, 520 Capdeville Street, New Orleans, LA 70130

This almost-hidden gem is located on Capdeville Street right off of Camp Street. It has eight beers on tap, as well as a nice bottle list. It offers a good mix of local craft beer, and other craft favorites like Sierra Nevada and Green Flash should make any beer geek happy. Without a doubt, get the Capdeville burger and some Green Flash West Coast IPA.

Rouses, 701 Baronne Street (at Girod Street), New Orleans, LA 70113

This Rouses, located in the CBD, has a great beer selection, and you can even pick up some sandwiches, tacos or pizza to go! I recommend the croque monsieur with some NOLA Hopitoulas. Located close to Lee Circle, this is a great place to pick up a quick sixer or case of your favorite brew for a parade during Mardi Gras.

Handsome Willy's, 218 South Robertson Street, New Orleans, LA 70112

This bar located in the CBD sits in what was once the infamous Storyville section of New Orleans, which was New Orleans' prostitution district. It is said that Handsome Willy's was once a house of ill repute called Jackson Inn, and the business is named after a pimp who once worked the premises. Now you'll find the less-exciting nurses and doctors from nearby Tulane Hospital, but the beer and tacos on Saints game days will make up for it.

Mid-City

The Bulldog, 5135 Canal Boulevard, New Orleans, LA 70124

This Bulldog branch is located in Mid-City and is a bit larger than the Uptown location. It offers the same great beer and food selection but with a much larger patio.

Bayou Beer Garden, 326 North Jefferson Davis Parkway, New Orleans, LA 70119

Located in an unassuming Creole double with neon everywhere, this bar looks like your neighbor is just throwing a party. It has a great draught and bottled beer selection with nice food options. I recommend the Disco Fries with an Abita Andygator. Or two.

Crescent Pie and Sausage Company, 4400 Banks Street, New Orleans, LA 70119

Pizza and beer will always be synonymous (it almost seems to be a recurring theme here). But this place isn't just a pizza shop. It's a Bart Bell–owned restaurant complete with Bad Bart's Black Jambalaya, pizza and a wide array of amazing sandwich options. In addition to a great craft beer selection, it also has house-made sausages.

Theo's Pizza, 4024 Canal Street, New Orleans, LA 70119

This pizza joint isn't your up-and-coming fancy pizza joint. It's old school—simple but great. With beers like NOLA Brewing and Green Flash, you can't go wrong. I recommend the Hawaii 5-0.

Finn McCool's, 3701 Banks Street, New Orleans, LA 70119

This Mid-City favorite is a must-visit when in town. Make sure you get the Deep Fried Truffle Mac N Cheese Balls. Nothing else matters. I don't even care what you drink. Just get them. You're welcome.

Juan's Flying Burrito, 4724 South Carrollton Avenue, New Orleans, LA 70119

Sometimes you want inexpensive beer and some tacos. Everybody loves tacos. This is the place for your taco and cheap beer fix. It's not a taco, but I recommend the Luau quesadilla with a PBR. Perfect hangover grub with a little hair of the dog.

Parkway Bakery, 538 Hagan Avenue, New Orleans, LA 70119

Parkway is your shrimp po'boy headquarters. You want beer with your po'boy? This place has it. Abita or NOLA would pair well and help you keep it local. Check out the old Jax and Regal Brewing breweriana on the wall as well.

METAIRIE

Lagers, 3501 Veterans Memorial Boulevard, Metairie, LA 70002

This place is like The Bulldog's younger ginger kid sister. Great beer selection, and it has crawfish banditos, too!

Phil's Grill, 3020 Severn Ave, Metairie, LA 70002

This is possibly one of the best burger joints in the area because you can create your own burger. It has a nice local beer selection, which pairs well with whatever burger creation you come up with.

Martin Wine Cellar, 714 Elmeer Avenue, Metairie, LA 70005

The Martin Wine Cellar in Metairie is the largest location and has the best beer selection. While you're at it, grab some grub! I recommend the boneless pork loin with some Havarti.

Dorignac's, 710 Veterans Memorial Boulevard, Metairie, LA 70005

There's an amazing beer selection at this locally owned grocery store located at the beginning of Veterans Boulevard, which I believe is the end of the parade route for the Metairie Mardi Gras parades.

New Orleans Beer

Whole Foods, 3420 Veterans Boulevard, Metairie, LA   70002

Again. It's a Whole Foods, but this is on the parade route. It has a great beer selection, and you can order sandwiches and stuff!

North Shore

(The North Shore is located across Lake Pontchartrain.)

The Barley Oak, 2101 Lakeshore Drive, Mandeville, LA   70448

The Barley Oak has a HUGE beer list with a great food menu. This is the place to drink good beer when on the North Shore!

Red, White and Brew, 120 East Thomas Street, Hammond, LA   70401

This Hammond wine store has turned into a great craft beer location for North Shore folks.

Acquistipace, 125 East Twenty-first Avenue, Covington, LA   70433

This Covington supermarket is one of the top craft beer locations in the state of Louisiana. Adam Acquistipace has done an amazing job curating one of the best beer selections in the state.

Westbank

(The Westbank is on the west bank of the Mississippi River, also referred to as Algiers—named after Algiers Point.)

The Crown and Anchor, 200 Pelican Avenue, New Orleans, LA 70114

Remember hearing about little bars nestled in old neighborhoods that you could just walk to? Yeah, this is that place. It offers a great beer selection with a wonderful mix of English and local beers—ciders, too! There are no food options, but you can bring some grub to the bar. My recommendation is to order from Gulf Pizza or get takeout from the Dry Dock Café just up the street.

Entrance to the Crown and Anchor in Algiers, Louisiana. *Jeremy Labadie.*

Old Point Bar Algiers, Louisiana. *Jeremy Labadie.*

Old Point Bar, 545 Patterson Drive, New Orleans, LA 70114

Another neighborhood bar located in Algiers Point, the Old Point is probably one of the most used locations for movies shot locally, having appeared in *The Expendables*, *The Green Lantern*, *Contraband* and *Bad Lieutenant: Port of Call–New Orleans*, among others. This bar is dog friendly and has live music almost every night of the week.

Note: Your special place might not be on this list. That doesn't mean it isn't cool enough or that something is wrong with it. It just means we didn't have enough room to add all the awesome places in New Orleans. New Orleans is a unique town with unique dining and drinking experiences. That's a whole 'nother book.

Chapter 6
TOURING THE EXISTING BREWERIES OF NEW ORLEANS

There are only eight brewery buildings left in New Orleans, not counting the two brewpubs. They are the Jax, Dixie, Falstaff, Union, Weckerling, Security, Louisiana and NOLA Breweries, and of these, Dixie is going to be torn down soon, quite possibly before this book makes it into print. Here's how to get to these historic buildings from the French Quarter. Keep in mind that you'll need a vehicle for this.

THE JACKSON BREWING COMPANY (JAX)

620 Decatur Street, across from Jackson Square

There's a miniscule museum of the brewery's history on the second floor, with enough memorabilia to keep you there at least five or ten minutes. The view over the river from the upper level is well worth it, though.

FALSTAFF AND DIXIE BREWING

Take Rampart Street uptown to Tulane Avenue and turn right. Proceed to South Tonti Street (six blocks past the Claiborne Avenue overpass; two blocks past the light at Galvez). On your right is either the remains of the Dixie Brewery or the lot it used to stand on. Dixie's iconic tower has been a major landmark of the city since 1907. It will be a shame to see it gone. Go two blocks farther on Tulane to South Dorgenois Street and take a left. Go slowly—Dorgenois is massively potholed. Proceed one block to Gravier. Ahead on your right is the Falstaff Brewery, now the Falstaff condominiums. Say hello to King Gambrinus.

Union Brewing

Getting to the Union brewery isn't difficult, but it is a little tricky. From the Quarter, take North Peters Street past Elysian Fields to Franklin Street and bear left. Go eleven blocks to North Robertson (five past St. Claude). North Robertson goes up a ramp on your right to get over the rail yard—don't take it. There's a service road just past the ramp on your right. Take it to Press Street, three blocks. The brewery is the four-story yellow brick building on your left.

Weckerling Brewery (now the World War II Museum) and Security Brewing

Exiting the Quarter on Decatur heading uptown, you will find that the street name changes to Magazine as you cross Canal. Take Magazine to Andrew Higgins.* The tall gray building on your right (on the downtown corner) is the World War II Museum, the former Weckerling Brewery. The pavilion attached is a recent addition. Take a left and go to the intersection of Andrew Higgins and Tchoupitoulas. You'll see Annunciation Street going off to your right. Turn left on Tchoupitoulas and go three short blocks to St. Joseph Street. Turn right (you have no choice about that, really). The first building on the right (rather pinkish) is Security Brewing. Its trademark is in the façade three stories up toward the left.

* Named after Andrew Higgins, the man who developed the landing crafts used in World War II, also known as Higgins Boats.

LOUISIANA BREWING AND NOLA BREWING

From the Quarter, take North Peters Street across Canal going uptown. The street name will change to one of the more famous of all New Orleans' streets: Tchoupitoulas (pronounced "Chop-i-TOO-lus"). Take Tchoupitoulas to Jackson Avenue (there is a part of this where Tchoupitoulas splits into two one-way sections; they come back together at Felicity Street, and you'll want to be in the right-hand lane to continue on Tchoupitoulas). There's a light at Jackson. At Jackson, look right. The massive old brick building just up from the corner is the Louisiana Brewery. There's not much to see of it, as the building is not accessible to the public. There is painted signage on the lake side of the building, though. Take Tchoupitoulas onward to Seventh Street. At Seventh Street, you will see a pair of dark red buildings on your right. This is NOLA Brewing. If it's a Friday shortly after noon, consider going in for the free tour and tasting. In any event, the taproom (toward the left side of the brewery) is open to the public Wednesdays through Mondays, as is the requisite gift shop.

PART III

LAGNIAPPE

CHAPTER 7

THE FIRST BEER TO BE DELIVERED BY AIR[89]

BY DONALD ROUSSIN AND KEVIN KIOUS
REPRINTED HERE WITH THE KIND PERMISSION OF THE AUTHORS

The William J. Lemp Brewing Company issued over 130 different postcards in the years preceding Prohibition. These postcards, some humorous, others featuring real photos, are avidly sought after by many collectors.

One of the rarer of the Lemp photo postcards shows a crowd of people standing in the brewery loading yard, off Cherokee Street, grouped around an early "glider"-type aircraft, not much advanced from the Wright brothers' machine that had made its maiden flight at Kitty Hawk less than a decade prior. A wooden beer bottle case marked "Brewed in the Brewery of Lemp" can be seen being loaded onto the airplane. The postcard carries the caption, "Falstaff is the first Bottled Beer to be delivered by aeroplane."

Another seldom-seen Lemp photo postcard shows the same airplane, now airborne, flying above the Lemp Brewery engine house. The postcard carries that same caption and, in addition, is marked "Circling the Lemp Smoke Stack."

Neither of these two postcards carries a date; no "from" or "to" information or other details of the flight.

However, there is a story behind the "The First Beer to be Delivered by Air" Lemp postcards. William J. Lemp Jr. was an early supporter of aviation and used its novelty value for advertisements, as well as for promotions of flying events he sponsored. These postcards were issued to celebrate the first delivery of beer via an airplane (at least as far as can be ascertained), which occurred in 1912. The following is an excerpt from a letter dated

LAGNIAPPE

September 22, 1967, addressed to the "Advertising Manager, Falstaff Brewing Corporation," from a John G. Shea, which tells, as they say, "the rest of the story":

> *Your advertising of Falstaff beer in the New York newspapers rings an ancient bell, which, I thought had long since been silenced by the years. Several years ago, as a professional writer on aviation history, I had an opportunity to chronicle the start of scheduled airplane transportation—which originated between St. Petersburg and Tampa, Florida, in 1914. Visiting St. Pete, I had the pleasure of meeting with Jay Dee Smith—an "early bird" airplane pilot, and mechanic to the Benoist aircraft used in the world's first scheduled airline operations.*
>
> *A chap by the name of Tony Jannus was the pilot of the first airline operation. Jannus was the Lindbergh of that era. He had established several altitude and long distance flying records prior to "settling down" to pilot the first Benoist "airliners." Now among his records was a flight in 1912, in a Benoist-type aircraft from St. Louis to New Orleans. And who sponsored this flight? The Lemp Brewery!*
>
> *Here's the rest of the story that you should be told before it gets lost in the labyrinths of time: Smith, who serviced the Benoist aircraft, followed Jannus down the rivers by land. The epic flight started at St. Louis with the Mayor, and various officers of the Lemp Brewery strapping a case of Falstaff bottled beer to the wing, behind the pilot's perch. Jannus was instructed to deliver the case of Falstaff to the Mayor of New Orleans. The flight was to be made in short, daily hops. First day out, Smith—upon meeting up with Jannus at a predesignated spot along the river—noticed the pilot was feeling no pain. Further observation revealed the case of beer had been broached—and Jannus was joyously engaged with the twelfth bottle.*
>
> *How about the Mayor of New Orleans? Smith inquired. No Problem, Jannus chortled.—Case flies much better empty!*
>
> *And that is why the Mayor or New Orleans almost lost his official aplomb while accepting an empty case of Falstaff beer. And now that all the principles are dead, until now, not a person in the Lemp, and later Falstaff Brewing Corporation, knew anything about this!*

Chapter 8
RECIPES—BECAUSE THIS IS LOUISIANA, AFTER ALL

Basic Crawfish Boil Recipe

Courtesy Scott Schwin

3.5 pound container of Zatarain's Crawfish Boil
½ cup cayenne pepper
2 crab boil bags
2 cups liquid crab boil
15 lemons cut in halves
12 onions cut in halves
12 cloves of garlic cut in halves
3 bunches of celery cut in quarters
35- to 45-pound sack of crawfish

Fill 100-quart crawfish pot about ¾ full of water and turn fire on. While water is heating up, add seasonings, squeeze lemons and add halves to water along with other vegetables listed above. If you would like potatoes in your boil now is the time to add them. While the water is heating up make sure to spray yourcrawfish with clean water to get as much mud off as possible.* Once the water is at a rolling boil add the crawfish and cover the pot again. This is also

---

* Some folks also put the sprayed-off crawfish into a (filled) kiddy pool to allow them to purge themselves. This works well but involves a lot more handling of the critters—which isn't always easy.

the time to add mushrooms and smoked sausage if you want to. Once the water has returned to a rolling boil, let it continue for 5 minutes and then turn off the fire. Let crawfish soak for an hour. Once you have cut the heat, this is a good time to put in frozen corn and frozen meatballs. This helps cool the water down, which forces the crawfish to soak up more flavor and gives you even more to eat! Use your garden hose to spray the sides of the pot to help with the cooling process. Be adventurous and try new things in your boil. Over my years, I have seen artichoke, Brussels sprouts, whole chickens, pork loins, whole hams, habanero peppers, asparagus, bell peppers, chicken wings and many other fun things to try. Just remember things like potatoes that take a long time to cook can go in at the beginning, while things like mushrooms and asparagus go in at the end or they will turn to mush.

(*Note from Argyle*: there are probably as many recipes for crawfish boil as there are cooks in Louisiana, all of whom have the best recipe—really, we do! Personally, I do this without quite so many seasonings: for a boil this size, one 3.3-pound container of Zatarain's Pro Boil will do nicely. I don't bother with the extra cayenne, the spice bags or liquids. As the spiced water heats, add red bliss potatoes, mushrooms, garlic heads, celery and onions [fresh pearl onions are great for this] and 15 lemons— squeeze them into the pot before you put 'em in. Chunked andouille sausage should go in now as well. I recommend the amazing andouille from Wayne Jacob's Smokehouse in La Place, Louisiana.[90] [It can't ship its products due to FDA regulations; it won't change its methods, nor should it. You'll need to go to Wayne Jacob's, and believe me, the trip is well worth it!] When the water comes to a boil, add the crawfish and cover the pot. When it all comes back to a boil, add frozen corn on the cob [cobbettes work best for this; fresh corn would be better, but corn and crawfish come into season at opposite ends of the calendar—more's the pity] and whatever other green vegetables you like. Kill the fire and hose down the outside of the pot. Let it all soak for no more than 12 minutes; you don't want to overcook the crawfish. Pull it all out [draining the liquid back into the pot], pour the food out onto a paper-covered table, squeeze 8 lemons and 4 oranges over the mass of food and let the feasting begin! Make sure you have enough paper towels and/or napkins, and have a trashcan handy for the mountain of shells you're about to generate! The second batch [cooked in the same liquid] will taste better than the first and the third better than the second. A crisp, hoppy beer is best with this: NOLA Blonde Ale, or even Hopitoulas or Abita's Jockamo IPA for those wanting a bigger beer.)

Bayou Teche Brewing's Brine for Poultry or Pork

Courtesy Bayou Teche Brewing

2 quarts beer (we usually use our Passionnée or Boucanée)
¾ cup salt
¾ cup brown sugar
½ cup Steen's cane syrup
4 teaspoons pink salt (a nitrate preservative available at sporting goods stores that sell cooking supplies to hunters)
1 tablespoon Tabasco sauce
Fresh (not dried) thyme, green onions, bay leaves, sage, juniper berries, whole black peppercorns (you can't go wrong, just add a bunch of these or other herbs)

Put all the ingredients in a pot, bring to a simmer and stir to mix salt and sugar. Remove from the heat and allow to cool, then refrigerate until chilled.

Add your meat (duck or chicken breast or other pieces, thick pork steaks, what have you). Refrigerate for 10 hours in brine—you might need to weight them down with a plate or bowl on top. Remove the meat from the brine and place on a rack in the fridge for about 6 hours (up to overnight) to dry.

Smoke the meat in a hot smoker for several hours (2 to 3); we usually like to bring the meat up to an internal temperature of 165 degrees Fahrenheit.

Braised Chicken Mole Po' Boy with Spicy Cilantro Aioli and Crispy, Perfect Tin Amber–Battered Onion Rings

Courtesy Jay Ducote from Bite and Booze

For the mole and braised chicken:
1 dried chipotle chili
1 dried ancho (poblano) chili
1 dried mulato chili

1 dried pasilla chili
2 tablespoons sesame seeds
2 tablespoons pecans, chopped
6–8 chicken thighs (roughly 4 pounds, skin on, bone in)
Kosher salt and freshly ground black pepper
3 tablespoons peanut oil
1 medium yellow onion, finely diced
4 tablespoons (about 1.5 ounces) semi-sweet chocolate or Mexican chocolate,
  chopped
¼ teaspoon ground cinnamon
⅛ teaspoon ground cloves
2 cloves garlic, minced
1½ cups chicken stock
1½ cups (12-ounce can) Tin Roof Perfect Tin Amber Ale
1 ripe tomato or 3 to 4 plum tomatoes, roughly chopped
1 tomatillo, husked, rinsed and roughly chopped
2 tablespoons golden raisins
½ teaspoon dried thyme
1 tablespoon sugar

Preheat an oven to 350 degrees Fahrenheit.
Pull out stems and remove seeds from all chiles. Tear them open if necessary
to scrape out seeds. Place all chiles on baking sheet and place in oven for 5
minutes until fragrant. When cooled, finely chop the chiles and place aside.

Spread out sesame seeds and chopped pecans on the same baking sheet
and put into the oven to toast for 10 to 12 minutes until the sesame seeds
have turned a toasted brown color. Set aside.

Season the chicken with salt and pepper on both sides.

In a cast-iron skillet or Dutch oven, place the peanut oil over medium-
high heat. Sauté the onions until sweated, about 5 minutes and then
add the chopped chiles. Add a little salt and pepper to season. Reduce
heat to medium. Continue cooking for another 3 minutes or so, stirring
with a wooden spoon or spatula. Add the chocolate, cinnamon, cloves
and garlic and stir over heat until chocolate is melted. Add the chicken
stock and beer and stir to incorporate. Add the tomato, tomatillo, toasted
sesame seeds, toasted pecans, raisins, thyme and sugar. Simmer for 30
minutes and taste. Adjust salt and pepper if necessary. Remove skillet
from heat and allow to cool slightly. Place the mole in a blender or large
food processor and puree until smooth, about 1 minute. Return the mole
to the skillet or Dutch oven and return to a simmer. Place the chicken
into the mole in one layer, ensuring that each piece is coated in sauce.

Braise the chicken in the sauce for half an hour, flipping each piece once through the cooking process. Again, remove the skillet from the heat and transfer the chicken to a work surface or baking pan. Allow to cool and then separate all the meat from the bones and skin. Shred the meat and return it all to the mole again to keep it warm.

For the spicy cilantro aioli:
1 large egg yolk
1 tablespoon Creole mustard
2 cloves garlic, minced
1 cup olive oil, divided (not extra virgin, if using extra virgin, cut it with grape seed oil or canola oil)
1 tablespoon lemon juice plus 1 teaspoon lemon zest
2 tablespoons green onion (no white parts), finely sliced
1 fresh jalapeno, seeded and minced
$\frac{1}{4}$ teaspoon crushed red pepper flakes
$\frac{1}{4}$ cup cilantro leaves
Kosher salt and freshly ground black pepper

In a mixing bowl, place the egg yolk, Creole mustard and a pinch of salt. Whisk together until combined and you see ribboning (trails in the yolk when whisking). Add 1 clove of minced garlic. Slowly drizzle in $\frac{3}{4}$ cup of the olive oil while whisking to emulsify with the egg yolk. Add lemon juice and continue to whisk. If necessary, add just a teaspoon of water to help with consistency. Add a little freshly cracked black pepper and taste.

In a food processor, add the lemon zest, green onion, jalapeno, remaining garlic clove, crushed red pepper flakes, cilantro, a little salt and pepper and the other $\frac{1}{4}$ cup of olive oil. Blend to combine. Pulse if necessary. Add a little extra olive oil if needed.

Place the mixture from the food processor in the mixing bowl with the aioli. Whisk to combine the two together. Taste and adjust seasoning with salt, pepper or lemon juice if desired.

For the beer-battered onion rings:
6–8 cups frying oil (peanut, canola, etc.)
2 eggs, beaten
$\frac{1}{2}$ cup corn meal
$\frac{1}{2}$ cup all-purpose flour, plus more for dredging
$\frac{1}{2}$ cup Perfect Tin Amber Ale
$\frac{1}{4}$ cup whole milk
2 teaspoons Cajun/Creole seasoning such as Slap Ya Mama
1 large yellow onion cut into $\frac{1}{4}$- to $\frac{1}{2}$-inch rings

Heat the oil in a heavy pan to 360 degrees Fahrenheit. In a medium mixing bowl, whisk the two eggs until they are beaten. Add the corn meal, flour, beer, milk and seasoning and continue to whisk until it is all incorporated. Dredge the onion rounds in flour and then shake off the excess. Dunk them in the beer batter and then place them into the hot oil. Fry in batches, turning occasionally, until golden brown, three to four minutes, then remove from oil and place them on a paper towel–lined plate.

For dressing the po' boy:
6 French bread po' boy loaves
2 cups iceberg lettuce, shredded
2 tomatoes, thinly sliced

Slice a piece of French bread in half length-wise. On the bottom part, spoon a heaping scoop of braised chicken and mole sauce and spread it evenly over the bread. On top of the chicken, add shredded lettuce and tomato slices. Top that with several rounds of beer-battered onion rings. On the top half of the po' boy bread, spread the spicy cilantro aioli. Place that on top of the onion rings and enjoy!

Brew Dat Crock Pot Roast Beef Po' Boy

By Jeremy Labadie

For the roast:
1 yellow onion
1 tablespoon minced garlic
2 bottles Abita Turbodog
3.5 pounds shoulder roast

Cut up the onion and place it in the bottom of crockpot with garlic. Add one bottle of Abita Turbodog to the crockpot. Open the other bottle and drink it. Sear roast on all sides and add to crockpot. Cook for 11 hours.

For the gravy:
½ cup of flour
1 tablespoons Tony Chachere's Creole Seasoning

Remove the roast from the crockpot. Pour all juice and drippings into a separate pan. Stir in ½ cup flour into the broth and turn the heat to medium high. Stir with a wire whisk until the flour has thickened and the gravy is smooth. Continue to cook slowly to brown the flour and stir constantly. Add Tony Chachere's to the gravy; season the gravy to taste.

Shred the roast and put back into the crockpot. Pour gravy over the roast and mix well. Enjoy on fresh Leidenheimer's* bread.

Buddha's Temptation

By Craig Giesecke

6 ounces balsamic vinegar
3 slices bacon
6 dried apricots
2 ounces blue cheese crumbles

Put vinegar in a sauté pan at medium heat to a boil. Your goal is to reduce it to the consistency of maple syrup—takes about 10 minutes.

Cut each slice of bacon in half, making six. Stuff apricots with the blue cheese and then wrap each apricot with a piece of the bacon. Secure bacon by putting all six apricots on a wooden skewer or individually with toothpicks. Deep-fry at 350 degrees Fahrenheit or in a pan half filled with hot oil until bacon reaches desired doneness. Drizzle with the reduced vinegar. Pairing: NOLA Brown Ale.

---

*Leidenheimer's is a local New Orleans bakery that produces an extremely light bread and is a staple for making po' boys. Any sufficiently light bread will work if push comes to shove. Using an otherwise delicious, dense baguette is kind of missing the point here. Roast beef po' boys are usually sloppy to eat! Be prepared to go though a bunch of napkins. (At the Parkway Bakery, there's a sign outside reading, "If our po' boys had any more heritage, you'd need more napkins!" Just sayin'…)

DRUNKEN CARAMELIZED FIG JAM WITH ABITA ABBEY ALE

By Natalie Parbhoo

3 cups fresh Louisiana figs (or any fig if you can't get this variety), stems cut and halved (about 1½ pounds)

½ cup granulated sugar

¼ cup dark brown sugar (Sugar will equal ¾ cup total in mixture below, or you can use all of one type of sugar. Do not use sugar substitute! That will not set the jam.)

½ teaspoon lemon zest

½ teaspoon or large pinch kosher salt

½ cup water

Mix together ingredients and let sit at least 1 hour or overnight

In a pot, pour in 12 ounces (1 bottle) of Abita Abbey Ale or another beer of your choice—use a malty brown ale. A Belgian dubbel, trippel or quadrupel will work well, as would a wee heavy as these types of ales contain many similar flavor profiles with the figs. They will also add a deep, satisfying touch to the sweet jam. There's a very slight bitterness that lingers in the background that balances the jam perfectly once the ale has boiled down, making a jam that's not overly sweet and also very complex.

Put the fig mixture in the pot of beer and bring everything to a boil. Squeeze half a lemon into the mixture. You can also use an orange (the high pectin content in the citrus helps it thicken and adds a brightness that complements the figs). Total juice should be 2 to 3 tablespoons.

Add a small pinch of ground cloves.

Cook on low for at least 20 minutes and up to an hour, until it becomes dark and almost sticky, caramelizing the sugars. Stir occasionally to make sure the bottom sugars do not scorch and then add ½ cup water, bring to another low boil and simmer until fig mixture is thick.

You can add or subtract any of the amounts of sugar, lemon zest, lemon juice and beer—every batch is different. Toward the end, taste and tweak it accordingly to your desire. This recipe is not overly sweet, so you may want it sweeter; if you do, add sugar to water in a separate cup or bowl. Make sure you dissolve the sugar, whether its on the stove or in a microwave, and then add it back to the pot or else you'll have grainy jam.

NEW ORLEANS BARBECUED SHRIMP

Courtesy of Steve Schmitt

Note: New Orleans–style barbecued shrimp is a distinctive dish that actually has very little to do with what we think of as barbecue, outside of the fact that it is cooked over coals on a grill. It originated at Pascal's Manale restaurant on Napoleon Avenue over fifty years ago. This is a rather more evolved version.

5 pounds fresh large head-on shrimp
2 Meyer lemons (or 3 regular ones, or even 3–4 limes), crosscut in half
6–10 strands fresh rosemary (about 60 inches total stem length)
1 head of garlic, cloves peeled and lightly crushed
Creole seasoning, such as Slap Ya Mama or Tony Chachere's
Seafood barbecue seasoning, such as Paul Prudhomme's Seafood Magic
Lea & Perrins Worcestershire sauce
Cayenne pepper
Spanish hot pimenton (smoked paprika)
Olive oil
Beer (use a lighter beer for this; NOLA Blonde Ale works well)
Hot sauce, Tabasco or Crystal, depending on how sharp a flavor you want
    (Crystal is mellower)
1 pound butter, unsalted
Fresh baguettes
Many napkins

Fire the coals up and let them settle until white. Put the shrimp into an aluminum roasting pan as they are, heads, shells and all. Squeeze the citrus over the shrimp; if you like a stronger citrus flavor, leave the squeezed fruit in the pan. Add the rosemary and garlic cloves. Season with Creole seasoning, seafood barbecue, Lea & Perrins, cayenne and pimenton to taste—go by instinct. Drizzle generously with the olive oil; add 14 ounces or so of beer. Add enough hot sauce to your taste—be generous. Slice the butter ¼-inch thick and put on top of it all. Drink the remaining beer.

Put the pan on the coals and cover until done—about 7 to 10 minutes. Serve directly with the bread for a peel-and-eat feast! A hoppy beer is called for, same as with a crawfish boil.

Lagniappe

If you want to do a truly decadent twist on this, make a barbecue beurre blanc. When you pull the shrimp off the fire, strain the liquid into a smallish pan and reduce it by half. Add some cream (no more than 3 or 4 tablespoons) and whisk in whole butter to make the beurre blanc sauce. You'll need at least 3 times as much butter as liquid, but this is well worth it!

NOLA Irish Channel Stout Floats

Courtesy Brenton Day from www.thealerunner.com

3 tablespoons Bailey's Irish Cream
3 tablespoons heaving whipping cream
4 ounces NOLA Irish Channel Stout
2 scoops vanilla ice cream

Stir together Baileys, cream and NOLA Irish Channel Stout in a measuring cup. Fill a 10- to 12-ounce glass with ice cream halfway. Pour the stout mixture over the ice cream slowly. Do the same for as many servings as you wish. Drop in a spoon or straw and enjoy.

North Texas Red

Adapted from Glenn Waggoner's article "How to Throw a Chili Party," Esquire magazine, page 34, January 1983, which was in turn based on the book A Bowl of Red, by Frank X. Tolbert. You'll need a huge kettle, a small saucepan and a large skillet to make this. This makes enough for 35–40 chili-heads.

1 pint tequila (for establishing and maintaining a proper chili perspective)
15 ancho chilies, seeded and deveined
10 Japanese chilies, seeded and deveined
3 chipotle chilies, seeded and deveined
10 jalapeno chilies, seeded and deveined
30 cloves garlic, roughly chopped
½ cup bacon drippings (or vegetable oil, if you must)
30-pound beef chuck roast, diced about 1 inch

105

1 cup flour
4 cups commercial chili powder
6 cups beef broth (if you have homemade stock, use that instead of canned)
3 quarts beer (use a lighter beer for this, maybe Abita Light or Golden)
6 tablespoons cumin seeds
4 tablespoons dried oregano
4 tablespoons ground coriander
1 tablespoons sugar
Salt to taste (start with 2 tablespoons)
No onions
No beans
No tomatoes

Have a big hit of tequila to set your mental stage. (Pace yourself, though; while cooking chili isn't brain surgery, you'll still need your wits.) In the small saucepan, cover the dried chilies with water and bring to a boil. Simmer for 15 minutes, and then cover the pan and let it sit off the heat.

Chop the jalapenos into small bits and set aside.

Take another hit of tequila.

Lightly sauté the garlic in bacon drippings (or oil) in the skillet over medium heat—do not brown. Transfer to the kettle.

Brown the meat a handful at a time in the skillet. Turn it frequently; don't add too much at a time to keep from steaming. Transfer to the kettle as you go. This is boring and messy—be prepared to clean up a lot of spatters.

Sift the flour and chili powder together and add to the browned meat. Stir it all well, until the meat is evenly coated.

Put the rehydrated chilies and their liquid into a blender along with the jalapenos and puree them. Add to the kettle.

Add beef broth and 2½ quarts of beer to the kettle. Stir well and bring to a boil over medium heat. Stir often to keep it from sticking. The liquid level should be 2 to 3 inches above the meat; add more beer if necessary, even water if you must.

More tequila, chase with remaining beer.

Reduce the heat to a strong simmer, stir in the remaining seasonings and sugar. Cook, stirring as needed, until the meat just begins to fall apart—about 3 hours. Taste and adjust the seasonings as needed.

Tequila.

If you like the flavor of masa harina (and if you prefer the chili to be a bit thicker), make a slurry with 4 to 5 tablespoons of masa harina and a cup of cooking liquid. Add to the pot and cook another 15 minutes, stirring all the while. (This is optional.)

Cool the chili in shallow pan(s) and refrigerate overnight.
Finish the tequila, if you haven't already.

The following day, skim the fat off the chili and let it warm up a bit on the counter for an hour or two before heating it up (SLOWLY!) on low heat (or even covered in the oven; set it at 200 degrees Fahrenheit if you do that). In any event, stir to make sure it doesn't stick and burn. When it's hot, serve it up!

Serve whatever you like with the chili: flat bread, rice, chips, bean salad, corn salsa, guacamole, diced tomatoes and/or onions, cheese, sour cream—literally, whatever. And beer—the fuller-flavored, the better. NOLA Mechahopzilla or Hopitoulas, Abita Andygator (or even their Amber!), Tin Roof's Rougarou—anything sufficiently excessive.

TIN ROOF BLONDE SMOKED GOUDA AND CHEDDAR SOUP

Courtesy Brenton Day from www.thealerunner.com

½ pound bacon
1 medium onion, chopped
2 cloves garlic, minced
2 cans Tin Roof Blonde Ale
2 cups chicken stock
2 cups red potatoes, diced
4 cups heavy cream
1½ pounds smoked Gouda cheese, shredded
½ pound sharp cheddar cheese, shredded
2 tablespoons cornstarch
1 tablespoon Worcestershire sauce
Salt, black pepper and cayenne pepper to taste
Green onions or chives, chopped

In a large stockpot, fry bacon until crisp. Remove, drain on paper towels and crumble into bits, setting aside. Add chopped onion and sauté with bacon drippings. Once clear, add garlic and cook until colorless. Add 2 cans of Tin Roof Blonde Ale and chicken stock, bringing to a simmer. Add potatoes, stir well and then cover and simmer for 15 minutes, or until potatoes are cooked. Reduce heat and slowly add heavy cream while constantly stirring. Fold in the cheese in small batches and stir to melt while ensuring not to overheat. Add cornstarch to thicken up the soup. Slowly raise heat to melt cheese. If necessary, add more beer to achieve desired thickness and then stir in Worcestershire and salt and pepper to taste. Serve with crumbled bacon bits and onions/chives as garnish.

CHAPTER 9

BREWING TERMINOLOGY

adjuncts. Adjuncts are other sources of fermentable sugars added to the basic grains, used both for flavor and economics. They are typically used in mass-produced American lagers. Adjuncts range from rice and corn to even honey or syrup.

alcohol by volume (ABV). A measurement of the alcohol content of a solution in terms of the percentage volume of alcohol per volume of beer. This measurement is always higher than alcohol by weight and is the basis of taxation. To calculate the approximate volumetric alcohol content, subtract the final gravity from the original gravity and divide by 0.0075. For example: $1.050 - 1.012 = 0.038/0.0075 = 5$ percent ABV.

alcohol by weight (ABW). A measurement of the alcohol content of a solution in terms of the percentage weight of alcohol per volume of beer. For example: 3.2 percent alcohol by weight equals 3.2 grams of alcohol per 100 centiliters of beer. This measure is always lower than alcohol by volume. To calculate the approximate alcohol content by weight, subtract the final gravity from the original gravity and divide by 0.0095. For example: $1.050 - 1.012 = 0.038/0.0095 = 4$ percent ABW. This measure is handy for determining your blood alcohol concentration and thus whether or not you should be driving at the moment.

ale. An ale is a beer that is fermented using a top-fermenting yeast. It is usually fermented at warmer temperatures than lager. Stouts, IPAs and Pale Ales all fall into this category. Local examples: NOLA Mechahopzilla, Bayou Teche LA31, Abita Amber, Tin Roof Blonde.

barley. A cereal grain derived from the annual grass *Hordeum vulgare*. Malted barley is used as the primary grain in the production of beer and certain distilled spirits (Scotch whiskey, notably), as well as a food supply for humans and animals.

bitterness. In beer, bitterness is caused by the tannins and iso-humulones of hops. Bitterness of hops is perceived in the taste. The amount of bitterness in a beer is one of the defining characteristics of a beer style.

bomber. A bomber is a twenty-two-ounce bottle of beer.

bottle conditioning. This is a process by which beer is naturally carbonated in the bottle as a result of fermentation of additional wort or sugar intentionally added during packaging. This is also how Champagne is carbonated.

bottom fermentation. One of the two basic fermentation methods, characterized by the tendency of yeast cells to sink to the bottom of the fermentation vessel. Lager yeast is considered to be bottom fermenting compared to ale yeast that is top fermenting. Beers brewed in this fashion are commonly called lagers or bottom-fermented beers.

Brettanomyces. A type of yeast and more specifically a genus of single-celled yeasts that ferment sugar and are important to the beer and wine industries due to the sensory flavors they produce. Brettanomyces, or "Brett" colloquially, can cause acidity and other sensory notes often perceived as leather, barnyard, horse blanket and just plain funk. These characteristics can be desirable or undesirable. It is common and desirable in styles such as Geuze, Lambic, Oud Bruin, several similarly acidic American and Belgian styles and many barrel-aged styles. It is also a hallmark of Chateau Musar wines.

brew kettle. A brew kettle is the vessel used during the brewing process where the wort (unfermented beer) is boiled.

carbonation. This is the process of introducing carbon dioxide into a liquid (such as beer) by:

1. pressurizing a fermentation vessel to capture naturally produced carbon dioxide;
2. injecting the finished beverage with carbon dioxide (also called Charmat process);
3. adding young fermenting beer to finished beer for a renewed fermentation (krausening);
4. priming (adding sugar to) fermented wort prior to packaging, creating a secondary fermentation in the bottle, also known as "bottle conditioning." This is also referred to as "methode traditionale" in Champagne.

carboy. A carboy is a large container used for fermentation, typically made of glass or plastic. A carboy usually holds five to six gallons and is the preferred default working container for most U.S. home brewers.

cask. A barrel-shaped container for holding beer. Like wine barrels, casks are frequently made of oak staves and bound by iron bands. Kegs, by comparison, are usually made of stainless steel, fiberglass or aluminum.

cask conditioning. Storing unpasteurized, unfiltered beer for several days in cool cellars at about forty-eight to fifty-six degree Fahrenheit (thirteen degrees Celsius) while conditioning is completed and carbonation builds. It is considered superior to bottle conditioning.

contract brewing company. A business that hires another brewery to produce some or all of its beer. The contract brewing company handles marketing, sales and distribution of its beer, while generally leaving the brewing and packaging to its producer brewery. Two examples of this would be the Minhas Craft Brewery in Monroe, Wisconsin (which currently produces Dixie), and the F.X. Matt brewery of Utica, New York.

craft brewery. According to the Brewers Association, an American craft brewer is small, independent and traditional.

•Small: Annual production of beer is less than six million barrels. Beer production is attributed to a brewer according to the rules of alternating proprietorships. Flavored malt beverages are not considered beer for purposes of this definition.

•Independent: Less than 25 percent of the craft brewery is owned or controlled (or equivalent economic interest) by an alcoholic beverage industry member who is not himself a craft brewer.

•Traditional: A brewer who has either an all-malt flagship (the beer that represents the greatest volume among that brewer's brands) or has at least 50 percent of its volume in either all-malt beers or in beers that use adjuncts to enhance rather than lighten flavor.

dry hopping. The addition of hops late in the brewing process to increase the hop aroma of a finished beer without significantly affecting its bitterness. The primary benefit of dry hopping is the addition of otherwise fugitive elements of hop flavoring that would otherwise be lost by volatilization.

fermentation. The chemical conversion of fermentable sugars into approximately equal parts of ethyl alcohol and carbon dioxide gas through the action of yeast. The two basic forms of fermentation in brewing are top fermentation, which produces ales, and bottom fermentation, which produces lagers.

fresh hopping. The addition of freshly harvested hops that have not yet been dried to different stages of the brewing process. Fresh hopping adds unique flavors and aromas to beer that are not normally found when using hops that have been dried and processed per usual. Synonymous with wet hopping.

growler. A jug- or pail-like container once used to carry draft beer bought by the measure at the local tavern. Growlers are usually a half gallon (sixty-four ounces) or two liters (sixty-eight ounces) in volume and made of glass. Brewpubs often serve growlers to sell beer to go. Often a customer will pay a deposit on the growler but can bring it back again and again for a refill. Growlers to go are not legal in all U.S. states.

hopping. The addition of hops (either fresh or dry) to either un-fermented wort or fermented beer.

hops. A perennial climbing vine, also known by the Latin botanical name *Humulus lupulus*. Native to northern Europe, hops have been a staple for brewing beer since the ninth century.

international bitterness units (IBU). The measure of the bittering substances in beer (analytically assessed as milligrams of isomerized alpha acid per liter of beer in ppm). This measurement depends on the style of beer. Light lagers typically have an IBU rating between five and ten, while big, bitter India Pale Ales can have an IBU rating between fifty and seventy.

lager. A lager is a beer that is fermented with bottom-fermenting yeast at colder temperatures. A local example of a lager is Dixie.

lagering. Storing bottom-fermented beer in cold cellars at near-freezing temperatures for periods of time ranging from a few weeks to years, during which time the yeast cells and proteins settle out and the beer improves in taste and clarity.

lagniappe. Lagniappe is a small gift given a customer by a merchant at the time of a purchase; broadly, it is something given or obtained gratuitously or by way of good measure, as in a baker's dozen. Also, "a little something extra."

Laissez le bon temps rouler. A Cajun expression meaning "Let the good times roll."

lautering. The process of separating the sweet wort (pre-boil) from the spent grains in a lauter tun or with other straining apparatus.

lauter tun. A large vessel fitted with a perforated false bottom (like a colander) and a drain spigot in which the mash is allowed to settle and sweet wort is removed from the grains through a straining process. In some smaller breweries, the mash tun can be used for both mashing and lautering.

malt barley. Barley or other grains that have been steeped in water, allowed to germinate and then dried (either in kilns or over open fire, as for making Rauschbier) for the purpose of converting the insoluble grain starches to soluble substances and sugars.

mash. A mixture of ground malt (and possibly other grains or adjuncts) and hot water that forms the sweet wort after straining.

mashing. The process of mixing cracked malt (and possibly other grains or adjuncts) with hot water to convert grain starches to fermentable sugars and non-fermentable carbohydrates that will add body, head retention and other characteristics to the beer. This is done by the action of alpha and beta amylase enzymes, which catalyze the hydrolysis of starches to sugars. Mashing also extracts colors and flavors that will carry through to the finished beer and provides for the degradation of haze-forming proteins. Mashing can require several hours and produces a sugar-rich liquid called wort.

mash tun. The vessel in which grist is soaked in water and heated in order to convert the starch to sugar and to extract the sugars, colors, flavors and other solubles from the grist.

microbrewery. As defined by the Brewers Association, a microbrewery is a brewery that produces fewer than fifteen thousand barrels of beer per year with 75 percent or more of its beer sold off-premise.

package. A general term for the containers used to market beverages. Packaged beer is generally sold in bottles and cans. Beer sold in kegs is usually called draught beer.

Prohibition. A law instituted by the Eighteenth Amendment to the U.S. Constitution (stemming from the Volstead Act) on January 18, 1920, forbidding the sale, production, importation and transportation of alcoholic beverages in the United States. It was repealed by the Twenty-first Amendment to the U.S. Constitution on December 5, 1933. The Prohibition era is sometimes referred to as the Noble Experiment.

Rauschbier. A style of beer characterized by the use of smoked malt; a German-style beer noted for being well suited for accompanying smoked meats. A good local example is NOLA's Smoky Mary.

sour. A taste perceived to be acidic and tart, sometimes the result of a bacterial influence intended by the brewer, from either wild or inoculated bacteria such as lactobacillus and pediococcus.

sparging. Rinsing the mashed grains to extract the last remaining sugars for the wort. This is done in a lauter tun.

wort. The sugar solution obtained by mashing the malt. Wort is usually boiled with hops to impart the hops' qualities to the resulting beer.

yeast. A single-cell eukaryotic microorganism, classified as fungi. Certain of them are highly beneficial to us. During beer's fermentation process, yeast converts the natural malt sugars into alcohol and carbon dioxide gas. Yeast was first viewed under a microscope in 1680 by the Dutch scientist Antonie van Leeuwenhoek; in 1867, Louis Pasteur discovered that yeast cells lack chlorophyll and that they can develop only in an environment containing both nitrogen and carbon.

AFTERWORD

When we moved to New Orleans in 2006, the city was just starting to recover from the ravages of Hurricane Katrina. The Road Home program was getting a lot of airtime and newspaper coverage but didn't apply to us newcomers. There was a lot of talk about what had been lost and whether or not New Orleans *would*, in fact, recover—not to mention about how the recovery would proceed and how thorough it would be. It was also debated whether the city should be rebuilt at all. The debates about which neighborhoods would be rebuilt and which ones would not (or should not) raged in the press and in town meetings on an almost daily basis, with particular emphasis on race, economic class and social justice. We also ran into a local meme—"Dey ain't dere no more"—which seems to have been an ongoing thing here since forever. Faulkner was quite right: the past isn't dead; it's not even past.

Researching brewing history here seems to be an exercise in loss. While finding out stuff is fun, a large part of the research is discovering just how little is left. When I started this project, I just wanted to know about New Orleans brewing in a historical context. I found out very quickly just how much was gone; in some cases, not just the buildings but whole streets. This led me to a whole raft of other questions. For instance, what did the beer made at the Marais Street Star Brewery taste like? It brewed in the heart of Storyville from 1869 until 1886, yet on the 1893 Sanborn map of New Orleans, it is shown as a small, forlorn lot labeled "abandoned brewery." Today, that location is part of the Iberville public housing project. There's no indication that anyone ever brewed there. Seventeen years of brewing, and then gone—erased without a trace. George Auer's Eagle Brewery ran for just one year longer, until 1887. No one alive today knows what his beer tasted like. To me, this is simply heartbreaking.

We like to preserve things, to make the past sustainable in the present in spite of the universe doing everything possible to tear down the old and bring on the new. Sometimes we can do this and make it work. The Weihenstephan Brewery in Freising, Bavaria, is one good example;* Jens Bangs Stenhouse in Aalborg, Denmark, is another.† But when a brewery or winery shutters its doors, a piece of our edible culture goes away, and we usually don't get it back. Given a recipe to work with, we can reconstruct a dish or a beverage from times past. I have done so many times over the years,‡ and the results have been fascinating (not to mention tasty). On the other hand, any such reproduction is still only an educated guess—and we don't have the original to compare it to.

While I have the names, dates and most of the locations of the historic New Orleans brewers, what I don't have is the formulas they used or descriptions of the beers themselves outside of the names on the labels. As for the flavors, you'll just have to use your imagination—or do some research…

---

* It has been brewing weissbier since AD 1046, twenty years before William the Conqueror took off to conquer Great Britain. Here's a link to its website: http://weihenstephaner.de/language.php.

†Built in 1624 and still in use by the family, it has never been sold. It has a great restaurant (Duus) in the basement that has plaques from every U.S. Coast Guard unit that has visited there. It also makes great mead. Here's a link to its website: http://www.visitdenmark.com/jens-bangs-stenhus-gdk596534.

‡ I have made hundreds of dishes and brewed several dozen ales and meads from medieval cookbooks with great success. This is relatively easy to do, as we have the books to work from. *The Closet of the Eminently Learned Sir Kenelm Digbie, Kt.* is a great one to start with, should you be interested in this sort of thing. Digbie died in 1665; the book was published in 1669. Chiquart's treatise on fourteenth-century Savoyard cookery is another great one (Chiquart was the Duke of Savoy's chief cook in the 1500s and wrote his book then; he was not a scholar doing the research after the fact).

NOTES

PREFACE

1. The name was changed to Jax in 1956, the name having been purchased from the Jax Brewery Jacksonville, Florida, when it went out of business. Having a brewery named Jax on Jackson Square was probably just too much of a good thing to pass up, and it had a good run.
2. http://www.metrojacksonville.com/article/2007-aug-jax-beer-the-drink-of-friendship.
3. Racontoursinnola.com.
4. http://www.amazon.com/American-breweries-Dale-Van-Wieren/dp/096461670X.
5. http://goo.gl/maps/OJ9Br.
6. Nicholas Schmidt's brewery is listed at "Philip n. Annunciation" in *Gardner's Directory of New Orleans*, 1861. No building shown near there is labeled as a brewery (active or not) on any map I have yet found, so it's an open question.
7. http://www.beerbikemunich.com/index.html. This is one of many seen in Munich.
8. http://beerandwhiskeybros.com/2011/05/10/pedal-til-you-puke-beer-bikes-are-awesome.

CHAPTER 1

9. Adrian Block and Hans Christiansen had a brewery in the Dutch New Amsterdam colony from 1612 until 1623.

10. http://www.frankenmuthmuseum.org/timeline.pdf

11. The German People of New Orleans, 1850 – 1900, John F. Nau, PhD, 1958

12. http://www.schaefer-beer.com/history/default.aspx; http://en.wikipedia.org/wiki/F._%26_M._Schaefer_Brewing_Company.

13. http://en.wikipedia.org/wiki/Frederic_Tudor.

14. http://en.wikipedia.org/wiki/Ice_house_(building).

15. http://en.wikipedia.org/wiki/John_Gorrie.

16. *Ice and Refrigeration Illustrated.*

17. Merrill, *Germans of Louisiana*, 150.

18. Ibid., 147–50.

19. http://en.wikipedia.org/wiki/Anheuser-Busch_InBev.

20. http://en.wikipedia.org/wiki/Prohibition; http://en.wikipedia.org/wiki/Prohibition_in_the_United_States.

21. http://en.wikipedia.org/wiki/Tied_house.

Chapter 2

22. Christovitch et al, *New Orleans Architecture*, 15.

23. http://books.google.com/books?id=DwYhzS32sfUC&pg=PA15&lpg=PA15&dq=brasserie+brewery+new+orleans+1727&source=bl&ots=3wzxEpNfAp&sig=ULcl8PNymXWDbC2m-RkvarjlA40&hl=en&sa=X&-ei=0lWGUvb_B4qU2gX76YC4Bw&ved=0CDsQ6AEwAg#v=onepage&q=brasserie%20brewery%20new%20orleans%201727&f=false.

24. Merrill, *Germans of Louisiana*, 153.

25. Ibid., 147–50.

26. http://www.flickr.com/photos/wallyg/2484340991.

27. http://www.metrojacksonville.com/article/2007-aug-jax-beer-the-drink-of-friendship.

28. http://www.beerhistory.com/library/holdings/wagner_granitecity.shtml.

29. http://www.myneworleans.com/St-Charles-Avenue/July-2010/Remem-beer.

30. http://www.crescentcitybrewhouse.com.

31. http://en.wikipedia.org/wiki/Storyville; http://www.storyvilledistrictnola.com.

32. Baron, *Brewed in America*, 229.

33. http://www.nola.com/politics/index.ssf/2011/04/bayou_st_john_bridges.html.

34. http://en.wikipedia.org/wiki/Bernard_de_Marigny.

35. Nau, *German People of New Orleans.*

36. Sanborn Fire Insurance Company map of New Orleans, 1893.

37. http://louisianagenealogyblog.blogspot.com/2012/03/only-brewery-in-new-orleans-caspar.html#axzz2AtYoA1lo.

38. http://nolabrewhistory.com/breweries/columbia-brewery.
39. http://photos.nola.com/tpphotos/2011/09/175headline.html.
40. https://en.wikipedia.org/wiki/New_Orleans.
41. Merrill, *Germans of Louisiana*, 300.
42. http://www.bestofneworleans.com/gambit/new-orleans-know-it-all/Content?oid=1240705.
43. http://www.neworleansbar.org/documents/ENews07Nostalgia0912FirstDraft.pdf.
44. http://www.thecottonmillneworleans.com/history.
45. Merrill, *Germans of Louisiana*, 157.
46. Baron, *Brewed in America*, 266.
47. *Flynn's Digest of the City Ordinances*.
48. http://www.gordonbiersch.com.
49. Lafayette was annexed into New Orleans proper in 1852. https://en.wikipedia.org/wiki/New_Orleans.
50. http://louisianagenealogyblog.blogspot.com/2012/03/1866-new-orleans-brewerys.html#axzz2AtYoA1lo.
51. http://www.notarialarchives.org/robinson/atlas/robinson27.html.
52. http://www.gonola.com/2012/10/15/nola-history-beer-and-brewing-in-new-orleans.html.
53. http://www.nolabrewing.com.
54. http://familytreemaker.genealogy.com/users/l/a/q/Raymond-Laque-LA/WEBSITE-0001/UHP-0720.html.
55. http://www.neworleansbar.org/documents/DixieDoodlesArticle.6-15.pdf.
56. http://www.breweryage.com/pdfs/2000-11dixie.pdf.
57. http://nolabrewhistory.com/breweries/Dixie.
58. http://theneworleansblightblog.wordpress.com/2010/04/13/the-dixie-brewery.
59. http://www.byo.com/component/resource/article/Indices/16-Breweries/87-acadian-brewing-co.

CHAPTER 3

60. http://en.wikipedia.org/wiki/Homebrewing.
61. http://en.wikipedia.org/wiki/Abita_Brewing_Company.
62. http://www.covingtonbrewhouse.com/home.php.
63. http://bayoutechebrewing.com/about-us.
64. http://www.tinroofbeer.com/our-story.
65. http://www.chafunktabrew.com/Home/Story.
66. http://www.parishbeer.com/home.html.
67. https://www.facebook.com/pages/40-Arpent-Brewing-Company/325580000792452.

68. http://gnarlybarleybrewing.com.

69. https://www.facebook.com/pages/Mudbug-Brewery-LLC/242648455767926.

70. http://www.greatraftbrewing.com.

71. https://www.facebook.com/CajunFire.

72. http://lazymagnolia.com.

73. http://breweries.louisianatravel.com.

74. http://www.facebook.com/louisianacraftbeer.

CHAPTER 4

75. http://en.wikipedia.org/wiki/Ale_yeast#Warm_fermenting.

76. http://en.wikipedia.org/wiki/Ninkasi.

77. http://en.wikipedia.org/wiki/Hops.

78. http://en.wikipedia.org/wiki/The_Fens.

79. http://en.wikipedia.org/wiki/Malt.

80. http://en.wikipedia.org/wiki/Mashing.

81. http://en.wikipedia.org/wiki/Wort.

82. http://en.wikipedia.org/wiki/Small_beer.

83. http://en.wikipedia.org/wiki/Switchel.

84. http://en.wikipedia.org/wiki/Saccharomyces_pastorianus.

85. http://www.geneticarchaeology.com/research/500_years_ago_yeasts_
epic_journey_gave_rise_to_lager_beer.asp?utm_source=feedburner&utm_
medium=feed&utm_campaign=Feed%3A+GeneticArchaeologyNews+%2
8Genetic+Archaeology+News%29.

86 http://en.wikipedia.org/wiki/Lagering.

87. http://www.urbancincy.com/2010/05/queen-city-underground-tours-
through-otr-start-memorial-day-weekend.

CHAPTER 5

88. http://theavenuepub.com.

CHAPTER 7

89. http://www.beerhistory.com/library/holdings/lemp3.shtml.

CHAPTER 8

90. https://www.google.com/#q=wayne+jacob+smokehouse+laplace.

BIBLIOGRAPHY

Baron, Stanley. *Brewed in America: A History of Beer and Ale in the United States.* Boston: Little, Brown and Co., 1962.

Christovitch, M.L., Sally Evans and Friends of the Cabildo. *New Orleans Architecture: The Creole Faubourgs.* Gretna, LA: Pelican Publishing Company, 2006.

Flynn, J.Q. *Flynn's Digest of the City Ordinances, Together with the Constitutional Provisions, Acts of the General Assembly, and Decisions of the Courts Relative to the Government of the City of New Orleans.* New Orleans, LA: L. Graham and Sons, 1896.

Krebs, Roland, and Percy J. Orthwein. *Making Friends Is Our Business: 100 Years of Anheuser-Busch.* Privately printed, ca. 1953.

Merrill, Ellen C. *Germans of Louisiana.* Gretna, LA: Pelican Publishing Company, 2005.

Morris, Elli. *Cooling the South: The Block Ice Era, 1875–1975.* Richmond, VA: Wackophoto, 2005.

Nau, John F., PhD. *The German People of New Orleans, 1850–1900.* Leiden, LA: Mississippi Southern College, 1958.

Van Wieren, Dale P. *American Breweries II.* West Point, PA: East Coast Breweriana Association, 1995.

BIBLIOGRAPHY

ARTICLES

Gambit Weekly. "Blake Pontchartrain: The New Orleans Know-It-All." Several articles, no longer available.

Ice and Refrigeration Illustrated 20, nos. 1–6 (January–June 1901), Southern Ice Exchange (Google E-book).

WEB RESOURCES

http://freepages.history.rootsweb.ancestry.com/~neworleans

http://www.notarialarchives.org/robinson/guide.htm

http://nutrias.org/~nopl/house2/sanborn.htm (The Sanborn maps are also available online from Environmental Data Resources, which owns the maps. at http://www.edrnet.com.)

http://www.storyvilledistrictnola.com/

And of course, our good friends at Wikipedia for far more things than I have room right here to list (check the endnotes)

INDEX

INDEX

P

Pabst Brewing Company 32
Parish Brewing Company 56
Pearl 13, 32
Pelican 36, 37, 40, 42, 51, 52, 87
People's 34, 42, 52
Prohibition 27, 28, 33, 34, 39, 40, 41,
    42, 46, 48, 53, 54, 94, 113, 118

R

recipes 96
Regal 33

S

schenk 25, 26, 31
Schmidt, Nicholas 43, 51, 117
Security Brewing 42, 52, 89, 90
small beer 71
Soulé, Sebastian 38, 41, 51, 52
Southern Brewery 36
Stadtsbreuerei 31, 51
Standard 33, 40, 46, 52, 53
Star Steam 39
step-mashing 72
Storyville 16, 34, 35, 36, 83, 115
switchel 71

T

Tin Roof 56, 99, 107, 109
Tremé 16, 34, 35

U

Union 18, 28, 31, 34, 39, 42, 45, 51,
    52, 53, 89, 90

V

Valentine 35, 47
Volkmann, Ernest 39, 51

W

Weckerling Brewery 18, 40, 52, 53,
    89, 90

Weckerling, J.J. 32, 44, 52
World Bottling Company 39

ABOUT THE AUTHORS

Argyle Wolf-Knapp is a graduate of the Culinary Institute of America and a certified sommelier with the Court of Master Sommeliers. He has worked as a chef for over a decade in New York and currently works as a floor captain and supervisor at the famed Commander's Palace restaurant in New Orleans. Over the last thirty years, he has researched and reproduced various beers, ales, meads and foods from historical sources going back as far as Apicius. He's still a bit enamored by Elizabethan food and brewing. This is his first book.

Jeremy Labadie, aka the Beer Buddha, is a graduate of Tulane University. He has been on a continuous legal beer journey since 1996. He has a somewhat popular New Orleans beer blog called "The Beer Buddha," which he has been writing since 2008. He currently lives in New Orleans with his wife, Aaron, her three large dogs and their home-brew-loving seven-year-old daughter, Evangeline. This is his first and probably last book.

Visit us at
www.historypress.net
....

This title is also available as an e-book